"A CA
SEPARATION"

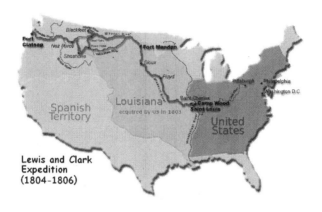

Lewis and Clark
Expedition
(1804-1806)

A COMPILATION OF

LECTURES BY

WARREN F. MUHAMMAD J.D.

1

FOREWORD

At the time of the publishing of this book, the movie "Get Out," written and directed by Jordan Peele, dominated the box office in its opening weekend. The film opens as an interracial couple, a black man, and a white woman, are getting ready to travel to her family's home in an upper class, lily-white neighborhood. Once the white woman's family meets this black man during the family gala, he is sized up physically and questioned as to his advantage as a black man in America. What he doesn't realize is that there is an unseen conspiracy by the white people at that gala to kidnap, hypnotize and essentially have his body and brain overtaken by them. Unbeknownst to this protagonist, he was one of many black men kidnapped, hypnotized and mentally and physical overtaken by this group of white people.

This movie is only a reflection of what the Original Man and Woman have experienced and endured for over four-hundred years in America. We have been kidnapped from our homeland; hypnotized into thinking that the white man and his interpretation of who God is will bring us salvation and grace; and finally indoctrinated by the system of white supremacy such that we can no longer think for ourselves. We are literally herded like sheep to our own destruction.

It is clear that the black cultural revolution is setting the stage for the black man and woman of North America and the world to awaken to the reality of their hypnotism, who they are and the need to set themselves apart from their oppressor.

On the back page of the Nation of Islam's newspaper, *The Final Call*, there is a list of twelve points of "What the Muslims Believe." Point number seven specifically states in part, "WE BELIEVE this is the time in history for the separation of the so-called Negroes and the so-called white Americans." However, point number nine clears up the reasons why the black man and woman must separate:

> WE BELIEVE that the offer of integration is hypocritical and is made by those who are trying to deceive the black peoples into believing that their 400-year-old open enemies of freedom, justice, and equality are, all of a sudden, their "friends." Furthermore, we believe that such deception is intended to prevent black people from realizing that the time in history has arrived for the separation from the whites of this nation.
>
> If the white people are truthful about their professed friendship toward the so-called Negro, they can prove it by dividing up America with their slaves. We do not believe that America will ever be able to furnish enough jobs for her own millions of unemployed, in addition to jobs for the 20,000,000 black people as well.

To understand what true separation is, we must parse and clear any misinterpretations of what it means to separate.

In defining separate as an adjective, Merriam Webster defines it as "forming or viewed as a unit apart or by itself. As a verb, separate is defined as "to cause to move or be apart" or divide or cause to divide into constituent or distinct elements. Finally, as a noun, separate is define as "things forming units by themselves, in particular."

Separation is "the act or process of separating" or "the state of being separated." In another definition, it is defined as "a point, line, or means of division; an intervening space." Finally, Webster defines separation as a "termination of a contractual relationship."

In this book, "A Case for Separation", Attorney Warren Muhammad has used the skills and expertise he learned as an anointed advocate for Freedom, Justice, and Equality to lay out the case and its arguments as to why the black man and woman of North America must "get out" and separate themselves from their oppressor and suppressor, physically, politically, mentally, and spiritually. Attorney Muhammad takes the reader not only into the historical and legal research to support his arguments, but he uses the foundational and fundamental core teachings of Master Fard Muhammad, the Honorable Elijah Muhammad, and the Honorable Minister Louis Farrakhan to show and prove at no limit of time that separation and independence from the rule and mind of white supremacy is the best and only solution.

Sis. Attorney Sadiyah Karriem

A CASE FOR SEPARATION

TABLE OF CONTENTS

A CASE FOR
SEPARATION

In the Name of Allah, the Beneficent, the Merciful, I bear witness that there is no God but Allah, who came and intervened in our affairs, in the person of Master Fard Muhammad, and that the Most Honorable Elijah Muhammad is his Messenger to us, but in fact is more than a Messenger but is the Exalted Christ and that the Honorable Minister Louis Farrakhan is their divine reminder among us. I greet you in our original Arabic language, the greetings of peace, As Salaam Alaikum.

The Honorable Elijah Muhammad said, in a Message to the Black Man;

> "it is far more important to teach separation
> of the blacks and whites in America than prayer".

Why would he say this?
What is so important about "Separation"?
Is he correct? Or is this an outmoded, outdated concept? Have we arrived at a point in our sojourn here in America where it is not necessary, or is it a concept worthy of analysis and consideration? What I intend to provide today is a brief sketch of an analysis for our consideration. We shall take a look at the concept of separation historically, politically and scripturally. May Allah purify my thoughts and guide my words.

I start with a Scriptural Question asked in (Isaiah 49: 24) "Shall the prey be taken from the mighty, and shall the lawful captive be delivered?"

I ask the question "What is a "Lawful Captive?"

Black African slavery had existed in the North American English colonies for 168 years before the U.S. Constitution was drafted in 1787. It had existed all across colonial America, but by 1804 most Northern states, finding that slavery was not profitable for them, had effectively abolished the institution. In the South, however, especially after the 1793 invention of the cotton gin, the institution grew, becoming an inextricable part of the economy and way of life.

The Bill of Rights, adopted in 1791, says nothing about slavery. But the Fifth Amendment guaranteed that no person could "be deprived of life, liberty, or property, without due process of law." Slaves were property, and slaveholders had an absolute right to take their property with them, even into free states or territories. The rhetoric in the Constitution and the Declaration of Independence about liberty, freedom, being created equal, and so on, was seldom considered applicable to blacks, slave or free. Seen a subservient race, they were excluded from consideration as members of society and had few rights. Section 2 of Article I states that apart from free persons "all other persons," meaning slaves, are each to be counted as three-fifths of a white person for the purpose of apportioning congressional representatives on the basis of population. Section 9 of Article I states that the importation of "such Persons as any of the States now existing shall think proper to admit," meaning, slaves would be permitted until 1808. And Section 2 of Article IV directs that persons "held to Service or Labour in one State, under the Laws thereof, escaping into another," meaning fugitive slaves, were to be returned to their owners.

You thought that the 13th Amendment ended "slavery," but the wording was so deceitful: *"Neither slavery nor involuntary servitude, except as a punishment for crime whereof the party shall have been duly convicted, shall exist within the United States, or any place subject to their jurisdiction."*

The 14th Amendment of the Constitution of the United States made us "lawful captives," for it states: *"All persons born or naturalized in the United States, and subject to the jurisdiction thereof, are citizens of the United States and of the State wherein they reside."* They declared us to be "citizens" without the rights of a citizen.

So we can see the mindset of the founding fathers was based on "separation", with one assigned the status of slave or non-citizen and the other, white, or master and citizen. What was our response?

SLAVE REBELLIONS!!!

San Miguel de Gualdape was the first European settlement inside what is now United States territory, founded by Spaniard Lucas Vázquez de Ayllón in 1526. It was to last only three months of winter before being abandoned in early 1527. The first group of enslaved Africans to set foot on what is now the United States were brought by Ayllón to erect the settlement. The employment of African slaves in the 1526 colony is the first instance of African slave labor within the present territory of the United States. Upon political disputes within the settlers, there was an uprising among the slaves, who fled to the interior and presumably settled with the Native American people. This incident is the first documented slave rebellion in North America. There is documentary evidence of more than 250 uprisings or attempted uprisings involving ten or more slaves. Three of the best known in the United States during the 19th century are the revolts by Gabriel Prosser in Virginia in 1800, Denmark Vessey in Charleston, South Carolina in 1822, and Nat Turner in Southampton County, Virginia, in 1831.

The historian Steven Hahn proposes that the self-organized involvement of slaves in the Union Army during the American Civil War composed a slave rebellion that dwarfed all others. Similarly, tens of thousands of slaves joined British forces or escaped to British lines during the American Revolution, sometimes using the disruption of war to gain freedom. For instance, when the British evacuated from Charleston and Savannah, they took 10,000 slaves with them. They also evacuated slaves from New York, taking more than 3,000 for resettlement to Nova Scotia, where they were recorded as Black Loyalists and given land grants.

Thus, we look at the case of Harry Jarvis. Born a slave on the eastern shore of Virginia, Jarvis took to the woods for several weeks after the Civil War began, where he survived owing to fellow slaves who brought him news and food. Then, seizing an opportunity, Jarvis headed to Fort Monroe, 35 miles away, where Union troops were stationed, and asked commanding General Benjamin Butler "to let me enlist." Although Butler rebuffed Jarvis and told him "it wasn't a black man's war," Jarvis stood his political ground responding, "I told him it would be a black man's war before they got through."

Prior to the civil war, there were many blacks involved in the abolitionist movement. You have heard much of Frederick Douglas, and others of his ilk, who took a somewhat conciliatory tone, but you may not have heard of others who called for resistance and open rebellion!

David Walker, 1785-1830

In September 28, 1829, David Walker published "Walker's Appeal, in Four Articles; Together with a Preamble, to the Coloured Citizens of the World, but in Particular, and Very Expressly, to Those of the United States of America", Written in Boston, State of Massachusetts,

"Fear not the number and education of our enemies, against whom we shall have to contend for our lawful right; guaranteed to us by our Maker; for why should we be afraid, when God is, and will continue, (if we continue humble) to be on our side? It is expected that all Coloured men, women and children, who are not too deceitful, abject, and servile, to resist the cruelties and murders inflicted upon us by the white slave holders, our enemies by nature. Beloved brethren--here let me tell you, and believe it, that the Lord our God, as true as he sits on his throne in heaven, and as true as our Saviour died to redeem the world, will give you a Hannibal, and when the Lord shall have raised him up, and given him to you for your possession, O my suffering brethren! Remember the divisions and consequent sufferings of *Carthage* and of *Hayti.* Read the history particularly of Hayti, and see how they were butchered by the whites, and do you take warning. The person whom God shall give you, give him your support and let him go his length, and behold in him the salvation of your God. God will indeed, deliver you through him from your deplorable and wretched condition under the Christians of America. I charge you this day before my God to lay no obstacle in his way, but let him go."

LISTEN TO HIS COURAGE!!!

"If any are anxious to ascertain who I am, know the world, that I am one of the oppressed, degraded and wretched sons of Africa, rendered so by the avaricious and unmerciful, among the whites. If any wish to

11

plunge me into the wretched incapacity of a slave, or murder me for the truth, know ye, that I am in the hand of God, and at your disposal. I count my life not dear unto me, but I am ready to be offered at any moment. For what is the use of living, when in fact I am dead."

Henry Highland Garnet,
"An Address to The Slaves Of The United States".

The National Negro Convention of 1843 was held in Buffalo, New York, drawing some seventy delegates a dozen states. Among the delegates were young, rising leaders in the African American community including Frederick Douglass, William Wells Brown, Charles B. Ray and Charles L. Remond. Twenty-seven year old, Henry Highland Garnet, a newspaper editor and pastor of a Presbyterian Church in Troy, New York, however captured most of the attention of the delegates with his "An Address to the Slaves of the United States" in which he called for their open rebellion. The speech failed by one vote of being endorsed by the convention. Garnet said, in part,

"In the name of God, we ask, are you men? Where is the blood of your fathers? Has it all run out of your veins? Awake, awake; millions of voices are calling you! Your dead fathers speak to you from their graves. Heaven, as with a voice of thunder, calls on you to arise from the dust... Let your motto be resistance! resistance! RESISTANCE! No oppressed people have ever secured their liberty without resistance.

What kind of resistance you had better make, you must decide by the circumstances that surround you, and according to the suggestion of expediency. Brethren, adieu! Trust in the living God. Labor for the peace of the human race, and remember that you are Four Millions."

AGAIN: OUR RESPONSE WAS "SEPARATION"
BLACK INDIANS

Runaway African slaves often found new homes in American Indian villages. Even though classified as "slaves" in White society, many African Americans became part of an INDIAN family group, and many intermarried with Native Americans - thus many later became classified as Black Indians. This is a unique history between African (black) slaves and Native American Indians, who are, themselves "Original People", which developed in many U. S. communities. There is scholarship existent, with factual support of records from Columbus onward, that support the contention that the initial "Atlantic Slave Trade" was the exportation of "Indians" of a dark color similar to "Ethiopians" to Europe and subsequently to Africa. This contention asserts that many so-called "African Americans" are actually descendants of "Black Indians" exported back from Africa to the West.

Crow Tribesman - 1873

THE WHITE MAN'S VIEW OF SEPARATION
THE AMERICAN COLONIZATION SOCIETY

The American Colonization Society (in full, The Society for the Colonization of Free People of Color of America), founded in 1816, was the primary vehicle to support the return of free African Americans to what was considered greater freedom in Africa. It helped to found the colony of Liberia in 1821–22 as a place for freedmen. Among its founders were Charles Fenton Mercer, Henry Clay, John Randolph, and Richard Bland Lee.

MIGRATION: BACK TO AFRICA

Most Englishmen and Anglo-Americans of this day felt that people of African descent were inferior to Europeans, even in the predominantly Calvinist and Quaker New England. Although slavery continued, prominent men like Presidents Thomas Jefferson and James Madison believed the emigration of Blacks to colonies outside the United States was the easiest and most realistic solution to the race problem in America.

In 1816, Paul Cuffee envisioned a mass emigration plan for African Americans, both to Sierra Leone and possibly to newly freed Haiti. Congress rejected his petition to fund a return to Sierra Leone. During this time, many African Americans began to demonstrate interest in emigrating to Africa, and some people believed this was the best solution to problems of racial tensions in American society. Cuffee was persuaded by Reverends Samuel J. Mills and Robert Finley to help them with the African colonization plans of the American Colonization Society (ACS), but Cuffee was alarmed at the overt racism of many members of the ACS. ACS co-founders, particularly Henry Clay, advocated exporting freed Negroes as a way of ridding the South of potentially 'troublesome' agitators who might threaten the plantation system of slavery. Other Americans also became active, but found there was more reason to encourage emigration to Haiti, where American immigrants were welcomed by the government of President Boyer. (Paul Cuffee)

Martin Robison Delany (May 6, 1812 – January 24, 1885) was an African-American abolitionist, journalist, physician, and writer, arguably the first proponent of American Black Nationalism. He became convinced, that the white ruling class would not allow deserving persons of color to become leaders in society, and his opinions became more extreme. His book, "The Condition, Elevation, Emigration, and Destiny of the Colored People of the United States, Politically Considered" (1852) Delany argued that blacks had no future in the United States. He suggested they should leave and found a new nation elsewhere, perhaps in the West Indies or South America.

In May 1859 Delany sailed from New York for Liberia, to investigate the possibility of a new black nation in the region. He traveled in the region for nine months. He signed an agreement with eight chiefs in the Abeokuta region that would permit settlers to live on "unused land" in return for using their skills for the community's good. It is questionable whether Delany and the chiefs shared the same concepts of land use. The treaty was later dissolved due to warfare in the region, opposition by white missionaries, and the advent of the American Civil War.

In April 1860 Delany left Liberia for England, where he was honored by the International Statistical Congress. One American delegate walked out in protest. At the end of 1860, Delany returned to the United States. The next year, he began planning settlement of Abeokuta. He gathered a group of potential settlers and funding. When Delany decided to remain in the United States to work for emancipation of slaves, the pioneer plans fell apart.

But there was also the position taken by many that the colonizing plan was a "trick" to rid America of the presence of "free" blacks, and only have black slaves in America" this position was clearly and eloquently stated by none other that "Richard Allen "Bishop of the African Methodist Episcopal Church In The United States."

> "We were stolen from our mother country, and brought here. We have tilled the ground and made fortunes for thousands, and still they are not weary of our services. But they who stay to till the ground must be slaves. Is there not land enough in America, or 'corn

enough in Egypt?' Why should they send us into a far country to die? See the thousands of foreigners emigrating to America every year: and if there be ground sufficient for them to cultivate, and bread for them to eat, why would they wish to send the first tillers of the land away? Africans have made fortunes for thousands, who are yet unwilling to part with their services; but the free must be sent away, and those who remain, must be slaves. I have no doubt that there are many good men who do not see as I do, and who are for sending us to Liberia; but they have not duly considered the subject--they are not men of colour. --This land which we have watered with our tears and our blood, is now our mother country, and we are well satisfied to stay where wisdom abounds and the gospel is free."

The Dawn of The Twentieth Century Saw The Continued Expression Of The Nationalist/Separatist Mind Still Vibrant.

MARCUS GARVEY

Marcus Mosiah Garvey, Jr., (17 August 1887 – 10 June 1940)[1] was a Jamaican political leader, publisher, journalist, entrepreneur, and orator who was a staunch proponent of the Black nationalism and Pan-Africanism movements, to which end he founded the Universal Negro Improvement Association and African Communities League (UNIA-ACL). He founded the Black Star Line, part of the Back-to-Africa movement, which promoted the return of the African diaspora to their ancestral lands.

NOBLE DREW ALI

Timothy Drew, calling himself the Prophet Noble Drew Ali, founded the Moorish Science Temple in 1913 in New Jersey. After some difficulties, Drew moved to Chicago, establishing a center there as well as temples in other major cities, where it expanded rapidly. In the late 1920s, journalists estimated the Moorish Science Temple had 35,000 members in 17 temples in cities across the Midwest and upper South.

BLACK NATIONALISM SINCE GARVEY

JOHN H. BRACEY, JR, states in his work, Domestic Colonialism and Black Nationalism:

> "Despite the beliefs, if not the desires, of most historians, black and white, black nationalism has deep roots in American History. Black Nationalism as a body of ideas and a pattern of behavior stemming logically from the colonial relationship of Black America to White America is both a response to colonial subordination and an affirmation of the existence of an alternative nationality and set of values. As Harold Cruse has remarked in his discussion of domestic colonialism: "It is not at all remarkable then that the semi-colonial status of the Negro has given rise to nationalist movements, It would be

surprising if it had not." This essay proceeds from the assumption that Black America is an internal or domestic colony and that an understanding of Black Nationalism is central to understanding the history of race relations in the United."

INTEGRATION: WHERE DID THIS COME FROM?

"The predominance of the integrationist ideology can be traced to a number of factors. First, the goals of integration and equal rights coincided with the interests of the new Negro middle class that was developing as a result, of the rise in trade union and low-level white collar jobs produced by an expanding postwar economy and the growth of federal, state, and local bureaucracies. This generation of clerks, teachers, and postmen had achieved a sufficient degree of economic security, to be able to direct their attention to issues such as integrated education, open housing, and free access to public accommodations, and they had the financial resources to support organizations like the NAACP, the Urban League, and the numerous local human relations committees that acted in their behalf. This group of blacks was making social and economic progress, and so far, as they were concerned, that meant all blacks were making progress.

Second, the publication of Gunnar Myrdal's An American Dilemma in 1944 set an ideological tone accepted by both black and white social scientists, who played important roles in protest movements and on human relations committees.

Who Is Gunnar Myrdal? Where Did He Come From? Why Is He Important? First, We Must Start With Andrew Carnegie

Andrew Carnegie, the great steel baron-turned-philanthropist, founded Carnegie Corporation of New York in November 1911. A page from the Carnegie website states, "At that time, the Corporation was the largest single philanthropic trust that had ever been established. With its original $135 million endowment from Mr. Carnegie, (equivalent to roughly $2 billion today), the Corporation has made grants totaling more than $1.4 billion. Andrew Carnegie envisioned Carnegie Corporation as a foundation that would "promote the advancement and diffusion of knowledge and understanding. In keeping with this mandate, our work incorporates an affirmation of our historic role as an education foundation but also honors Andrew Carnegie's passion for international peace and the health of our democracy."

In 1935, Frederick Keppel's (Carnegie Corporation President) adviser, Newton Baker, who had been mayor of Cleveland 1913-1916, and Secretary of War under Woodrow Wilson, questioned the foundation's policy of using the funds it devoted to issues of race to support "Negro" schools in the South. He argued that more needed to be understood about race, which was no longer just a southern problem, and that the Corporation should concern itself with the condition of blacks in northern cities (Jackson, Gunnar Myrdal and America's Conscience, p.17). He suggested that a study was needed to help the Corporation decide how to spend its money in such as way to have the most impact on the black minority. After a search through a list that included twenty-five names, Keppel chose Gunnar

Myrdal, the (white) Swedish economist, then thirty-nine years old. In the invitation to Myrdal, Keppel wrote that Carnegie Corporation wanted "someone who would approach the situation with an entirely fresh mind. We have also thought that it would be wise to seek a man in a non-imperialistic country with no background of domination of one race over another"

In 1944, Myrdal published the results of an exhaustive study on the plight of the Negro in America. "An American Dilemma" was a voluminous, pioneering work in sociology and cultural anthropology that systematically documented the bedrock of institutional racism under which African Americans still lived. Myrdal suggested that the NAACP could indeed mount a successful legal campaign to end school segregation. He offered that it was to the advantage of American Negroes, as individuals and as a group, to become assimilated into American society, and to acquire the traits held in esteem by the dominant culture. Education was the path to achieving this.

An American Dilemma emphasized integration as a goal and asserted that the black community and its institutions were pathological (Involving, caused by, or of the nature of a physical or mental disease) in nature and should be done away with and replaced by "normal" -that is, integrated -ones. He assumes that "it is to the advantage of American Negroes as individuals and as a group to become assimilated into American culture, to acquire the traits held in esteem by the dominant white Americans." Myrdal, with an eye on maintaining social stability accompanied by gradual, carefully defined changes, was opposed to an expansion in the size of the black population and, most of all, to the masses of blacks organizing themselves along racial lines. To justify such a view, the notion that most Americans believed in the American creed of equality of opportunity and in reward for individual merit was evoked as the framework within which blacks must carry out their struggle. The guilt feeling engendered in the white mind because of the gap between the rhetoric of the American creed and the reality of racial oppression would act as the prime motivating force.

BROWN V BOARD OF EDUCATION

The Supreme Court, in Brown v Board of Education took judicial notice of Myrdal's work, it forming part of the basis of the court's decision stating "and see generally Myrdal, an American dilemma (1944)." Chief Justice Earl Warren concluded, "separate educational facilities are inherently unequal. Even as he pushed the "civil rights" agenda, concomitantly, with Myrdal's "integrationist /assimilationist" ideology, Martin Luther King demonstrated an increasing awareness of the realities of race relations in America and the need for both unity and power in the black community!

THE INTEGRATION VS NATIONALISM

In "Where Do We Go From Here: Chaos Or Community?"
Dr. King relates a conversation with Stokely Carmichael:

"Stokely replied by saying that the question of violence versus nonviolence was irrelevant. The real question was the need for black people to consolidate their political and economic resources to achieve power. "Power," he said, "is the only thing respected in this world, and we must get it at any cost." Then he looked me squarely in the eye and said, "Martin, you know as well as I do that practically every other ethnic group in America has done just this. The Jews, the Irish and the Italians did it, WHY CAN'T WE? "That is just the point," I answered. "No one has ever heard the Jews publicly chant a slogan of Jewish power, but they have power. Through group unity, determination and creative endeavor, they have gained it. The same thing is true of the Irish and Italians. Neither group has used a slogan of Irish or Italian power, but they have worked hard to achieve it." This is exactly what we must do," I said. "We must use every constructive means to amass economic and political power. This is the kind of legitimate power we need. We must work to build racial pride and refute the notion that black is evil and ugly. But this must come through a program, not merely through a slogan."

He said also,

> "When a people are mired in oppression, they realize deliverance only when they have accumulated the power to enforce change. "

He said at another time

> "Our present urgent necessity is to cease our internal fighting and turn outward to the enemy, using every form of mass action yet known, create new ones, and resolve

never to let them rest. This is the social lever which will force open the door to freedom. Our powerful weapons are the voices, the feet and the bodies of dedicated, united people."

And finally, he said;

"More and more, the civil rights movement will become engaged in the task of organizing people into permanent groups to protect their own interest and to produce change in their behalf. This is a tedious task, which may take years, but the results are more permanent and meaningful. In the future, we will be called upon to organize the unemployed, to unionize the business within the ghetto, to bring tenants together into collective bargaining units and establish cooperatives for purposes of building viable financial institutions within the ghetto that can be controlled by Negroes themselves!

On the inside back page of the Final Call we find "THE MUSLIM PROGRAM". Under "What The Muslims Believe", Point No. 9 states:

9. "WE BELIEVE that the offer of integration is hypocritical and is made by those who are trying to deceive the Black peoples into believing that their 400-year-old open enemies of freedom, justice, and equality are, all of a sudden, their friends. Furthermore, we believe that such deception is intended to prevent Black people from realizing that the time in history has arrived for the separation from the whites of this nation."

"SOME OF THIS EARTH FOR OUR OWN OR ELSE!"

See Pages 2, 3 and 6

The Honorable Elijah Muhammad, Messenger Of Allah

Integration?
NO !

Separation?
YES !

Who Speaks For The So-Called Negro?

In *Message to The Blackman In America*, in the chapter "Program and Position," the Honorable Elijah Muhammad said, *"We do not believe that America will ever be able to furnish enough jobs for her own millions of unemployed in addition to jobs for the 20,000,000 Black people."*

Is this not the reality we see today? And you thought Elijah Muhammad was wrong! If you really want integration, here is what it really means!

Minister Louis Farrakhan in speaking on integration says,

"Within the word "integration" you'll find the prefix integer. What is an "integer"? In Mathematics, the meaning of an integer states: "The whole is equal to the sum of its parts," meaning you have to "belong to" in order to be "a part of." So, if I've got eight slices of bean pie, then I've got a whole pie! But if I've got six slices of bean, and two slices of apple, I don't have a "whole" pie, because the two parts that are apple don't belong with the six parts that are bean. So, if the whole is equal to the sum of its parts, you've got to belong to in order to be a part of."

SEPARATION IN INTERNATIONAL LAW
International Bill of Human Rights

Self-determination is recognized as a right of all peoples in the United Nations Charter, Universal Declaration of Human Rights, International Covenant on Civil and Political Rights and International Covenant on Economic, Social and Cultural Rights, known collectively as the International Bill of Human Rights. The Universal Declaration of Human Rights (UDHR), adopted by the United Nations General Assembly in 1948, recognizes that everyone has the right to a nationality and that no one should be arbitrarily deprived of a nationality or denied the right to change nationality. The UDHR also recognizes the right of everyone to freedom of thought, conscience, religion and expression including the freedom to hold opinions without interference and to seek, receive and impart information and ideas through any media and regardless of frontiers.

In the "Declaration on the Rights of Indigenous Peoples", Articles 3, 4 and 5 of the declaration read as follows:

> "Indigenous peoples have the right to self-determination. By virtue of that right, they freely determine their political status and freely pursue their economic, social and cultural development. Indigenous peoples, in exercising their right to self-determination, have the right to autonomy or self-government in matters relating to their internal and local affairs, as well as ways and means for financing their autonomous functions. Indigenous peoples have the right to maintain and strengthen their distinct political, legal, economic, social and cultural institutions, while retaining their right to participate fully, if they so choose, in the political, economic, social and cultural life of the State."

INDEPENDENT NATIONS

The following is a list of peoples who have recently become recognized as "Independent Nations" .

-March 21, 1990 - Namibia became independent of South Africa.
-May 22, 1990 - North and South Yemen merged to form a unified Yemen.

-October 3, 1990 - East Germany and West Germany merged to form a unified Germany after the fall of the Iron Curtain.

-September 17, 1991 - The Marshall Islands was part of the Trust Territory of Pacific Islands (administered by the United States) and gained independence as a former colony.

-September 17, 1991 - Micronesia, previously known as the Caroline Islands, became independent from the United States.

-January 1, 1993 - The Czech

-May 25, 1993 - Eritrea was a part of Ethiopia but seceded and gained independence.

-October 1, 1994 - Palau was part of the Trust Territory of Pacific Islands (administered by the United States) and gained independence as a former colony.

-May 20, 2002 - East Timor (Timor-Leste) declared independence from Portugal in 1975 but did not become independent from Indonesia until 2002.

-June 3, 2006 - Montenegro was part of Serbia and Montenegro (also known as Yugoslavia) but gained independence after a referendum.

-June 5, 2006 - Serbia became its own entity after Montenegro split.

-February 17, 2008 - Kosovo unilaterally declared independence from Serbia.

-July 9, 2011 - South Sudan peacefully seceded from Sudan following a January 2011 referendum. Sudan itself was the first to recognize South Sudan and did so one day early, on July 8, 2011.

Union of Soviet Socialist Republics

Fifteen new countries became independent with the dissolution of the USSR in 1991. Most of these countries declared independence a few months preceding the fall of the Soviet Union in late 1991.

Armenia
Azerbaijan
Belarus
Estonia
Georgia
Kazakhstan
Kyrgyzstan
Latvia
Lithuania
Moldova
Russia
Tajikistan
Turkmenistan
Ukraine
Uzbekistan

Former Yugoslavia

-Yugoslavia dissolved in the early 1990s into five independent countries.
-Bosnia and Herzegovina, February 29, 1992
-Croatia, June 25, 1991

- Macedonia (officially The Former Yugoslav Republic of Macedonia) declared independence on September 8, 1991 but wasn't recognized by the United Nations until 1993 and the United States and Russia in February of 1994

-

-Serbia and Montenegro, (also known as the Federal Republic of Yugoslavia), April 17, 1992 (see below for separate Serbia and Montenegro entries)

-Slovenia, June 25, 1991

SPECIAL CASE STUDY:
THE ESTABLISHMENT OF THE STATE OF ISRAEL

In the year 1897, at the summons of the spiritual father of the Jewish State, Theodore Herzl, the First Zionist Congress convened and proclaimed the right of the Jewish people to national rebirth in its own country. This right was recognized in the Balfour Declaration of the 2nd November, 1917, and re-affirmed in the Mandate of the League of Nations which, in particular, gave international sanction to the historic connection between the Jewish people and Eretz-Israel and to the right of the Jewish people to rebuild its National Home.

The catastrophe which recently befell the Jewish people - the massacre of millions of Jews in Europe - was another clear demonstration of the urgency of solving the problem of its homelessness by re-establishing in Eretz-Israel the Jewish State, which would open the gates of the homeland wide to every Jew and confer upon the Jewish people the status of a fully privileged member of the comity of nations. Survivors of the Nazi holocaust in Europe, as well as Jews from other parts of the world, continued to migrate to Eretz-Israel, undaunted by difficulties, restrictions and dangers, and never ceased to assert their right to a life of dignity, freedom and honest toil in their national homeland.

In the Second World War, the Jewish community of this country contributed its full share to the struggle of the freedom- and peace-loving nations against the forces of Nazi wickedness and, by the blood of its soldiers and its war effort, gained the right to be reckoned among the peoples who founded the United Nations.

On the 29th November, 1947, the United Nations General Assembly passed a resolution calling for the establishment of a Jewish State in Eretz-Israel; the General Assembly required the inhabitants of Eretz-Israel to take such steps as were necessary on their part, for the implementation of that resolution. This recognition by the United Nations of the right of the Jewish people to establish their State was deemed irrevocable.

WHY DO SOME PEOPLE BECOME INDEPENDENT STATES AND SOME NOT? RECOGNITION BY A GREATER POWER!!!!!

SEPARATION AND SCRIPTURE

GENESIS 15:12-14

[12] And when the sun was going down, a deep sleep fell upon Abram; and, lo, a horror of great darkness fell upon him. [13] And he said unto Abram, know of a surety that thy seed shall be a stranger in a land that is not theirs, and shall serve them; and they shall afflict them four hundred years; [14] And also that nation, whom they shall serve, will I judge: and afterward shall they come out with great substance.

ISAIAH 49:24-26

Shall the prey be taken from the mighty, or the lawful captive be delivered" but saith the lord, even the captives of the mighty shall be taken away, and the prey of the terrible shall be delivered: for I will contend with him that contendeth with thee and I will save thy children. And I will feed them that oppress thee with their own flesh; and they shall be drunken with their own blood, as with sweet wine; and all flesh shall know that I, the lord am thy Saviour and thy redeemer, the mighty one of Jacob.

HOLY QUR'AN 30:43

"Then set thyself, being upright, to the right religion before there come from Allah the day which cannot be averted: on that day they will be separated!

HOW CAN THIS HAPPEN?

ISAIAH 9:2

2 The people that walked in darkness have seen a great light: they that dwell in the land of the shadow of death, upon them hath the light shined.

ISAIAH 9:6-7

"For unto us a child is born, unto us a son is given: and the government shall be upon his shoulder, and his name shall be called wonderful, counselor, the mighty God, the everlasting father, the prince of peace. Of the increase of his government and peace there shall be no end, upon the throne of David, and upon his kingdom, to order it, and to establish it with judgment and with justice from henceforth-even forever. The zeal of the lord of hosts will perform this."

The seminal and cardinal base of the Nation of Islam is contained in Point Number 12 of What The Muslims Believe, which was stated on the back of the "Muhammad Speaks" newspaper and is on the back of "The Final Call"

WHAT THE MUSLIMS BELIEVE

Point No. 12-WE BELIEVE that Allah (God) appeared in the Person of Master W. Fard Muhammad, July 1930; the long awaited "Messiah" of the Christians and the "Mahdi" of the Muslims. We believe further and lastly that Allah is God and besides Him there is no God and he will bring about a universal government of peace wherein we can all live in peace together. "

So, with the coming of God in person to America, the Divine solution has been given to the centuries old problem of race in America. This is in fulfillment of the scripture, where it says in REV. 18:4-5:

"And I heard another voice from heaven saying, come out of her, my people, that ye be not partakers of her sins, and that ye receive not of her plagues. For, her sins have reached unto heaven, and God hath remembered her iniquities.

In "Message To The Blackman", The Honorable Elijah Muhammad said:

"I am not trying to get you to fight. That is not even necessary; our unity will win the battle! Not one of us will have to raise a sword. Not one gun would we

33

need to fire. The great cannon that will be fired is our unity. Our unity is the best. Why are you afraid to unite? Why are you afraid to accept Allah and Islam? It is only because the slave-master did not teach you of this! We must unite to ourselves as a nation of people."

The Honorable Elijah Muhammad built a nation within a nation right here in our midst. This was but a sign, because he said and knew that the nation would fall, because the principles on which it was built, while true, was "nearly correct". So, he said that although it would fall, it would rise again and never fall. He said that another man would be his helper and would get us all. The Honorable Elijah Muhammad said that Minister Louis Farrakhan was a "star" of unequalled brightness!!!

Minister Farrakhan has given us the framework for organizing our communities, for self sufficiency and survival. He has erected the structures through which self government can be attained through the "Nine Ministries" which he presented at the Tenth Anniversary of the Million Man March.

Ministry of Information

The Ministry of Information is the central agency which provides services that include the development of all sources for informing the public of the policies, plans and strategies necessary for the free flow and accessibility of information essential to an informed and empowered citizenry. This includes collection, research and dissemination of current events, history, analysis; the publication of books, pamphlets, magazines and use of the internet and social media. It is also responsible for the development of information systems and networks to secure internal and external communications, media program development and management and establishment of an office of media affairs and press secretary.

Ministry of Education

The Ministry of Education is responsible for the mental and moral development of the members of the society by means of formal instruction in a prescribed manner over a prescribed period of time in a system of learning ranging from pre-school through primary through advanced academic levels, culminating in the conferring of academic degrees, under the direction of a National Board of Education. In addition to academic instruction, students shall receive teaching and training in the way of righteous conduct, decency and self-respect, with the goal of making a better nation of people.

Ministry of Agriculture

The Ministry of Agriculture is responsible for the development and maintenance of a system of sustainable agriculture to provide wholesome, natural food to the members of society. In addition to food, this Ministry is responsible for the production of raw materials required to build good homes and manufacture clothing.

Ministry of Trade and Commerce

The Ministry of Trade and Commerce is responsible for the growth and development of the business and economic interests of the society. This ministry is dynamic in nature, relying on the input of consultants with experience and success in business and economics. It analyzes the economic state of the community and develops programs and policies for growth and stability on the basis of the needs of the community. It translates skills, talents and interests of the community into viable revenue streams and works with the Ministry of Education to encourage entrepreneurship.

Ministry of Defense

The Ministry of Defense ensures the safety, security and survival of the society and its members and develops policies and systems relating to the national security of the society, beginning with insuring safe and decent local neighborhoods. It is also charged with enhancement and protection of military and intelligence assets, structures and institutions.

Ministry of Justice

The Ministry of Justice protects the rights and privileges of the members of the society and provides for penalties to be imposed upon persons who violate or threaten to violate the law or disrupt the peace. No member of the community shall forfeit his or her rights and privileges of membership in the community without just cause and without due process in reaching a determination that such cause exists. This Ministry is charged with the development of an independent judicial system in order to carry out its charge. It also initiates legal action, including class actions, against external entities, including governments, corporations, institutions and/or individuals, who, through their actions, pose a threat to the essential rights of members of this community.

Ministry of Health & Human Services

The Ministry of Health and Human Services provides for the physical, mental and emotional well-being of the members of the society. The goal of the Ministry of Health is the fulfillment of the intention of the Creator for every human being to achieve his or her potential for both longevity and good health throughout life. Its efforts extend to the family and the community as well as the individual.

Ministry of Arts and Culture

The Ministry of Arts and Culture is the promotion of aesthetic, artistic and cultural expression in way that facilitates mental, emotional and moral upliftment of the members of the society. It includes visual and performing arts, including, but not limited to, music, film, dance, drama, literature, poetry, visual arts and sports. It includes promotion of theater companies, audio/video recordings, presentations, competitions and compilations and an annual Festival of the Arts. It extends to a wholesome sports culture for athletic competition and achievement.

The Ministry of Science & Technology

The Ministry of Science and Technology is the continuous development of technological resources, i.e., the application of scientific knowledge to the solution of human problems. This Ministry embraces the broad discipline of Engineering and its sub-disciplines, including civil engineering, the design and construction of public and private works, such as airports, roads, railways, water supply and treatment, bridges, dams and buildings. Also, chemical, electrical, aeronautical and mechanical engineering. This Ministry will also utilize information technologies to improve overall efficiency of all ministries, including the use of web sites and webcasts. This division will work closely with the Ministry of Information to develop standard IT protocols and operating procedures and encourage technological education and training.

Ministry of Spiritual Development

This Ministry bears responsibility for assisting the individual member of the community in the process of heeding truth and right guidance. Respect, honor and obedience to the Authority of the Creator in all aspects of life are essential to peace, harmony, freedom, justice and equality. In the words of the Honorable Minister Louis Farrakhan: *"...Self-development is an absolutely essential component of this microcosm of the new world. It is not enough that we grow horizontally through the acquisition of farms, factories, banks, industry, trade, commerce, money, good homes...horizontal growth alone is death. All dead things are on a horizontal level. Therefore, we must grow vertically: grow in uprightness, or we will be overcome by our horizontal growth."* The foundation of *this ministry are study and training units, "...designed on the Guidance of Allah(God) to produce: self-examination; self-analysis; self-correction and to quicken in each of us, the self-accusing Spirit. For it is only when we are awakened morally that we have to face the self-accusing spirit that leads to our resurrection." (from the lecture : "Self-Improvement: the Basis for Community Development", December 12, 1986.)*

In the lecture "Understanding The Nation Of Islam" the Honorable Minister Louis Farrakhan said. "this nation is for all of us!" He went on to say,

> "Come out of her my people," the voice from heaven said, "that you be not partakers of her sins and her plagues, for her sins have reached unto heaven." Go home with this question in mind: Are you willing to come out of this and come under the guidance of God? Jesus said, "I am the door." A doorway is for coming out of something and going into something. Jesus, the Messiah, the Mahdi, they want us to come out of the mind that produced the condition that we are in. He's the doorway out, but He's also the doorway in to a better world that represents the Kingdom of God. Is this just for Blacks? Are only Blacks suffering? Is this for our Latino family? Is this for Asians? Is this for Whites? Yes, it is, because when the Children of Israel went out, it was a mixed multitude that went out. So, those Whites that want to come out from under this, (Satan's World) take the door. Let's come out, unite and build a better world."

So, If You Hate White Supremacy This Is Your Nation If You Hate Black Inferiority, This Is Your Nation! If You Hate Oppression and Exploitation of Man Over Man, This Is Your Nation! If You Want to Live in A World Where All Men And Women Enjoy Freedom, Justice And Equality, This Is Your Nation!

HOLY QU'RAN SURA 2:127-128, Allah says,

"127 And when Abraham and Ishmael raised the foundations of the House: Our Lord, accept from us; surely Thou art the Hearing, the Knowing.[a] 128 Our Lord, and make us both submissive to Thee, and (raise) from our offspring, a nation submissive to Thee,[a] and show us our ways of devotion and turn to us (Mercifully); surely Thou art the Oft-returning (to mercy), the Merciful. Our Lord, and raise up in them a Messenger from among them who shall recite to them Thy messages and teach them the Book and the Wisdom, and purify them. Surely, Thou art the Mighty, the Wise. 129 Our Lord, and raise up in them a Messenger from among them who shall recite to them Thy messages and teach them the Book and the Wisdom, and purify them. Surely, Thou art the Mighty, the Wise."

A NATION SUBMISSIVE TO THEE, A NATION SUBMISSIVE TO GOD IS A "NATION OF ISLAM"!

THANK YOU FOR LISTENING, I LEAVE YOU AS I CAME BEFORE YOU WITH THE GREETING WORDS OF PEACE

AS SALAAM ALAIKUM!

THE AGE OF DISCOVERY

In the Name of Allah, the Beneficent, the Merciful, I bear witness there is no God but Allah, who came in the person of Master Fard Muhammad to whom all praise is due. I bear witness that Master Fard Muhammad met a man in Detroit. He came from his exalted place in the Holy Land to the bottom of Detroit, to find one person and he found that one man, whom we know now as, the Honorable Elijah Muhammad, but not only did he find Elijah Muhammad, Elijah Muhammad found him, because in his nature, in his being, he had been looking for God all his life and when he saw him, he said "I know who you are." When he heard his speech he recognized in his voice the God that he had been looking for all his life. So Master Fard Muhammad raised that black man as a Messenger to us and has exalted him as His Christ. Then he left in our midst another man who always looked for God, and always loved his people, and wanted to help his people. This one remains in our midst as a Divine Reminder for us and that one is the Honorable Minister Louis Farrakhan, and in their names I greet you in today's greeting words of peace, As Salaam Alaikum.

My subject today is "The Age of Discovery". At the Republican National Convention, (held in 2012) Clint Eastwood made the statement, "we own this country" (speaking to his audience). So, I ask, what does own mean? "Own", is a state or a fact of being an owner a legal right to possession. According to the Black law dictionary, "the complete dominion titled or proprietary right in a thing or claim. A "proprietary right." So, what is a proprietary right? A proprietary right means that the proprietor or owner is one who has exclusive title to a thing, one who possesses or holds title to a thing in his own right. So, Clint my question to you today is, where did white America gain title to this country? Where did they gain a proprietary right to this country? Since you say we own it? So, in order to properly analyze that, we must go back in history brothers and sisters.

The beginning of the Age of Discovery actually started back in 1452 with the Pope of the Catholic Church, Pope Nicholas V. He was dealing with the competing interests of Spain and Portugal, who were desiring to sail abroad, to sail the seas in discovery of foreign lands. Europe had become overcrowded. Well before it became overcrowded it was almost decimated by the black plague and the plagues, during what they call the Dark Ages. Eventually they started to come out of that and into the Renaissance. So, the Pope is trying to mediate this dispute so he issues what's called a Papal Bull or in Islam we may call it a Fatwa, right? He declares war on all Non-Christians throughout the world, specifically sanctioning and promoting the conquest and colonization and exploitation of Non-Christian nations and their territories. I'll read a little of it to you. This is called the Dum Diversas of 1452:

> "We grant to you full and free power through the Apostolic Authority of this edict to invade, conquer, fight, subjugate the Saracen, that was the European word for Muslims. The Saracen and Pagans and other infidels and other enemies of Christ and wherever established their kingdoms,

deities, royal palaces principalities and other dominions."

The Pope basically declared war on the Muslims and on everyone else of color in the world, and authorized the European army to go forth and capture, dominate, kill, take their goods, take their property, take their women, take their lands. So, it was on the basis of this edict, by the Pope, that Christopher Columbus, in 1492, sailed on behalf of Spain, and of course, he thought he was going to India but landed somewhere in the Bahamas. But, when he landed what did he do? He stepped off his boat walked through the water and planted a flag. And when he landed he said, " I am discovering this on behalf of the Queen of Spain", and shortly after that, John Cabot in 1497 sailed and landed in North America. So this became the basis of the British claim to North America. So, we have these folks showing up on land that is already populated. Already people there, there are animals and homes, people hunting and fishing and building and educating and raising their children and families, right for thousands of years but when they land they land on behalf of the sovereign that they sailed for and claim that land. And brothers and sisters this is called the Doctrine of Discovery. We are going to get more into that as we go forward, but this Doctrine of Discovery is going to be a doctrine, you will see, that has played out since 1452 and is still in effect today. So, now we have these colonies, in what's called North America and as you can see along the eastern seaboard there was the thirteen colonies.

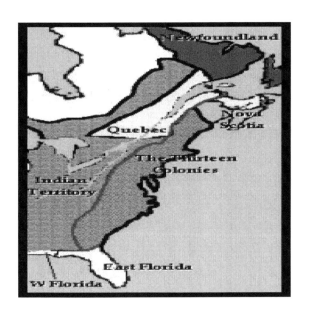

And then next to that is the Indian Territory. So, the British were negotiating with the Indian tribes, or nations, as we know them to be, and signing contracts of purchase. They were buying the land. They recognized that the Indians were there when they arrived, its common sense right? So, they were buying the land and they issued in 1763 the proclamation, it's called the Proclamation of Seventeen Sixty-Three. This came right at the end of the French and Indian war. Because as you see, you have Quebec up at the top (of the map) and France, was claiming part of this North American continent. Spain claimed part of it, and you have the British claiming part of it as well. So, there was a war, the French and Indian war, which ended in 1763. The French were defeated and left the North American continent except for what is now called Canada. So, as a consequence, Britain issued this proclamation that said no one is to cross this line between the thirteen colonies into Indian Territory. No one can go and buy land from the Indians but the British government. So, you had all these colonials, all in the thirteen colonies, and what they wanted more than anything was land. They could see all this land just over the border, just over the horizon, with fish and foul, and game and trees and fertile land. They could see it right there for the taking, yet, the King of England is saying you cannot go and get it. You can't even negotiate for it, you can't even buy it. And brothers and sisters, you've heard of the Boston Tea Party and the Stamp Act and all these reasons they have given us in our History classes in school, as to why Americans fought a revolution but they never told us it was about land. They never told us that it was these white folks in these colonies that wanted to go and take more, and more, and more, land and Britain was stopping them. And this was the primary motivating factor, and them deciding we have to fight to free ourselves for colonial authority, so we can own this land for ourselves. See now, they are not going to teach you that in the eighth-grade History class, they are not going to teach it in Masters History class. Praise to Allah! So now, we have this dilemma going on about this land issue in which, America fights his revolution and wins. Now, they form a government and they setup their Articles of Confederation and then the Constitution. The Constitution wrote in the fact that slavery was lawful until 1802, and then the only reason they wanted to make it unlawful was because they didn't want foreign countries importing slaves to America to compete with the local slave breading industry. So, it was more economical for the slave master to go among our women and produce slaves than it was to have them imported from abroad, and that is really the reason they illegalize the importation of slaves. Didn't find slavery unlawful, just the importation of slaves unlawful. So, there arose this dispute which is documented in the law

45

books in the case of Johnson vs. Macintosh. Johnson vs. Macintosh came about because some individuals, formed a land company, and entered into a purchase agreement with a group of Indians for millions of acres of land. They did it before the proclamation of 1763 and then after the proclamation they wanted to get a court to uphold their contract because they said that sure enough after 1763, individuals can't buy from the Indians, but we bought it before. So, there ensued this legal controversy. Now bear in mind, the people they bought the land from, it was like, let me see if I can give you an analogy, let's say we are here at the Mosque and a real estate agent pulls up in the parking lot, and there is a black guy who is just walking across the parking lot and they stop him and say sir, we would like to buy this land and this Mosque and he says well sure, how much you want to give me? He says I'll give you $25 and he says yeah where do I sign. He takes the $25 and walks on off, right. Then they come and tell us they own the property now. They bought it from someone who had no authority to even sell. In the same manner, these individuals bought it from a group of Indians who didn't even represent the tribe. To show you how real that is, later do you know the United States government entered into a contract with those who represented the tribe and bought it again. So, now you have this legal case between these individuals with the land company, and the government who is claiming ownership to the same land. So, the issue is who has the right to deal with the Indians. Well, this case came before Chief Justice John Marshall and John Marshall, made a decision. Chief Justice John Marshall observed that Christian European Nations had an assumed ultimate dominion over the lands of America during the age of discovery and that upon discovery the Indians had lost their rights to complete sovereignty as independent Nations. They only retained a right of occupancy in their land. In other words, the Indian nations were subject to the ultimate authority of the first nation of Christendom, to claim possession of the given region of Indian lands. So, when they show up, plant the flag, all of a sudden, now the Indian has lost the title to his own land. Just because the white man showed up. What kind of mind is this we are looking at? That's what I really want to get to with this speech, to look into the mind of these people. They will show up and say just because we are here, now you no longer own the land that you have been on for the last 16,000 years. You have a right to occupy it, you can continue to live on it, but we can distinguish your right to even live on it. That is the Doctrine of Discovery, now codified into the law of the United States of America. So, what happens then, Andrew Jackson becomes President and Congress pushes through the Indian Removal Act. So, how do they do it? The government would open up these land offices and they would issue warrants to individuals, or groups, and on the basis of the warrant, they would send out a surveyor. Here is a warrant that I found to a, what's his name, Mr. Penn, and on this warrant to Mr. Penn, this shall be your warrant to survey and lay off one or more surveys 200 acres of land.

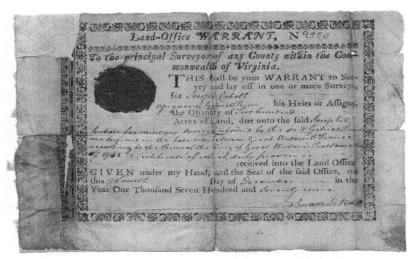

They are going to give it to him, I think he was an American Revolution War Veteran and they promised a lot the of war veterans in the American Revolution, you fight the revolution, we are going to go take the land and give you some. Ok, that is your compensation, so this is a warrant and the next thing they would do was to send out the surveyor, who on the basis of the warrant would take his instruments and survey the land and mark off the 200 acres. As part of the survey, he would describe the topography, the trees, the rivers the lake, the type of animals, and really lay it out so that this person would know what he is getting. What does this 200 acres consist of, how can I identify it when I get there. You know, how can I stake my claim to it. So, this was the job of the colonial surveyor, so they started going off into Indian Territory, on the basis of this document and surveying the land and marking it out for their ownership.

COLONIAL PEOPLE
The Surveyor
CHRISTINE PETERSEN

How many of you remember hearing about the Louis and Clarke expedition, we are all taught that in school. In 1804, President Thomas Jefferson sent Louis and Clarke on an expedition, which was basically a survey, and as you can see by the map, they had to cross the Louisiana territory that had just been purchased, cross into the Spanish territory and went all the way to the Pacific coast. But I don't remember them really telling us, or telling me about the fact that it was a survey based on the Doctrine of Discovery. Thomas Jefferson was well aware of the European Doctrine of Discovery, and wanted to send Louis and Clarke to map it out so that he could stake a claim as the first European to arrive there and have preeminence over any European country in the area. So again, here is the survey and it took years for them to make this trip and of course they described it and all of that.

So, on the basis of the Doctrine of Discovery, on the basis of surveying the land, to know what is there as I said before, they passed the Indian Removal Act in 1830, which led to the Trail of Tears. The Trail of Tears is a horrible, horrible story of the forced migration of our brothers. The Native American, the Red Man, from his homeland over into the barren lands of Oklahoma. Here is a photograph, and you can see, they are being escorted by the military; men, women, and children, thousands died on this Trail of Tears.

As they moved the Indians off the land, white people, the Americans, became emboldened in what they call Manifest Destiny. It's a term that was coined by a writer, a journalist named John L. O'Sullivan who said it was God's will that the Americans occupy the whole continent, their divine destiny called "Manifest

Destiny". In a column, which appeared in the *New York Morning News* on December 27, 1845, O'Sullivan addressed the ongoing boundary dispute with Great Britain in the Oregon Country, stating: "And that claim is by the right of our "manifest destiny" to overspread and to possess the whole of the continent which Providence has given us for the development of the great experiment of liberty and federated self-government entrusted to us." We see her a picture, I think this was on a stamp or something that they used back in those days that shows this Angel named Columbia going forth in front of the stagecoach bringing light to a land that is dark.

You see the darkness over here and you see the light behind her, the cloud of lights behind this white woman and the dark in front of her and as she proceeds forth across this American land she is bringing light. Again, it's the mindset, this is the mindset of the people we live with today. Manifest Destiny, it was their natural right. And here we have a map showing the lines of migration, of the Red Man from his native home.

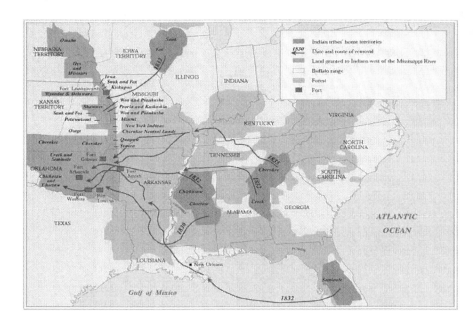

I want to point out something, let me walk over here, if you can see here, the white area, they say, according to this map, is Buffalo range and the Green area was forest and the Indians home territories are in the Orange. Well just like everywhere they found the best part to settle and then they used the rest for forestry, hunting, fishing and game and the buffalo, supplied their meat and built their homes or what have you, but if you look, this is Georgia, this area here is what's part of Alabama, Northern part of Georgia, and here you have what is now called Mississippi, this is the Mississippi River. So they wanted to push everyone across the Mississippi River so that they could occupy this fertile territory. Now, they had already begun to settle in these areas but this is the point I want to make. Why is this important to us? This removal of the Indians from their land over into Oklahoma. What does this mean to us? Why is this necessary? Why am I taking all of this time talking about the Indians? Why is this so important, they are our brothers but what does that have to do with our lives? With our history? You know why is it so important to know that in 1832 the Chickasaw and the Choctaw were forced out of Mississippi. I'm going to bring it home, real close to home, in my own home. This ladies name is Isabella.

Isabella Fitzgerald, this is my grandmother, my father's mother, her maiden name was Isabella Barnes and I have gone back and talked to my mother about this, and verified what I am about to show you. I didn't know Isabella, she died when I was a small child, maybe I was 2 or 3 years old. I don't have a recollection of her, but I always knew of her, her husband's name was Gus and that is all I ever knew about Isabella. She is my grandmother. I didn't know where she came from, how she got to Houston or anything. Another little side story, when I was a child my father bought me a dog, a boxer dog, and to this very day the boxer is my favorite dog, because this dog was like a family member to us. She was my best friend in many ways. And the dog's name was Missy, my Daddy named her Missy and Missy was loved by all of us. When Missy finally got hit by a car, we had a funeral for Missy. We buried Missy in the back yard with a full funeral. But during my research I consulted my good Brother, Attorney Ronald Ray, a brilliant researcher on genealogy and the family tree. He helped me to find members of my family that I didn't know existed, I didn't know anything about. And through our searches Ron found this document, this is an 1880 census and it shows the name at the top, you will see Missy Barnes.

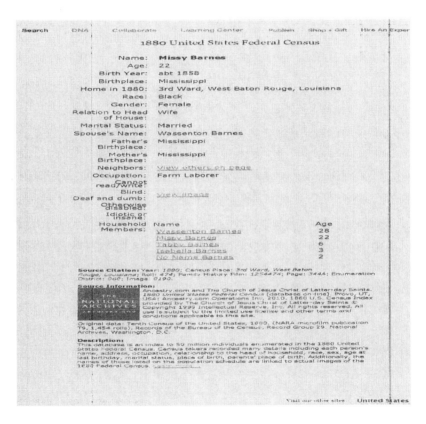

54

Missy! She was 22 years old, her birth date was about 1858 and she was born in Mississippi. If you look down at the bottom, I don't know if you can see it very well, how household members were. There's Washington Barnes 28, that's her husband and Missy Barnes 22, you have Tabby Barnes but should be Toby, Tabby Barnes was 6 and Isabella was 3. Missy Barnes, Isabella's Mother is my Great Grandmother on my Father's side who was born in Mississippi in 1858. So now I realize that my Great Grandmother was born into slavery, in the 1850s in Mississippi and this was possible in large part because the Indians had been removed from the land in the 1830's which opened up the expansion in the Mississippi territory by white people coming in to claim land and bring their slaves. So, this is why, this is important to us brothers and sisters, this is why we have to study the 17,000,000 plus the 2,000,000 Indians. Praise to Allah! So, to summarize this Doctrine of Discovery, first there had to be a discovery, somebody had to show up. It didn't matter if anybody was already there, just show up. This is the European concept of this Doctrine of Discovery, and upon showing up, bing, we own it. Next, was the actual occupancy and current possession. Once they showed up, they started to build forts and settlements so that they could lay claim to their ownership. Next was preemption, in other words, preemption means our title now supersedes any preexisting title. Because we showed up and we built a home or settlement here now we own the title, as against the original occupants and again anybody else who will show up. So, if the French showed up we are already here, it's ours and also no one could deal with the Indians but the European who claimed this right of Discovery. Native title was no longer any good. Title now vested in the discoverer, and then there is a concept called Terra Nullius, which means if the land is vacant we claim it. Not only if the land is vacant, if there are people living there and they are not living according to the standards of civilization of the Europeans, we take it. I mean you are sleeping in tepees, they say you need to have log cabins for houses. You are educating children under their fathers or their uncles, they say you need schools, that's not the European level of civilization. So, under Terra Nullius if you are not using, or if you are not using it to their pleasure, they own it. Christianity, if you are not a Christian, you are out. This law is for Christians only. Again civilization, these savages have to be civilized. Ok, so that's just a brief overview of what this Doctrine of Discovery means. So, what has this meant going forward? This Doctrine of Discovery has resulted in the total domination of the entire world. South America, Africa, Asia, The Pacific Rim, he went all over the world under his Doctrine of Discovery, claimed it and then went in and subdued it militarily. This Doctrine shapes the political configuration of the world as we know it today. Nigeria was not Nigeria 1,000 years ago. It was something else. There were the empires of the Mandinka and the Songhai and Mali and Ancient Ghana. But now Nigeria is a land that consists of three distinct groups with about 200 different languages, and they cannot get together because they were cobbled together by Britain who drew their political boundaries. This Doctrine of Discovery has enabled, or in his mind justified, the entire domination of the entire world and they did it through a law. Now you know the Holy Qur'an says, you read it all the time, it says, Their Evil was made fair seeming. So, even though they were stealing the land, killing the inhabitants, they concocted and erected this legal structure to make it lawful in their own eyes, to make their evil fair seeming. There is a concept called The Intertemporal Law. Now Intertemporal Law is an international law concept where treaties are analyzed to determine the continuation of their validity, whether they are still valid or not. So, let's say a treaty was entered into 50 years ago, and now things have changed and you want to look at the treaty and determine whether or not the treaty is still valid between nations. Well, according to Intertemporal Law, it says that changes in international law after the formulation of the treaty and changes in the meaning of expressions in the treaty, that's what they are looking at, the existence of a right, must be determined based on the law at the time of the creation of the right, and the international law applicable to the continued existence of the right. Are ya'll with me? This is the framework that law is looked at now, today in the International Courts of Law. You look at the treaties between the Indians and the European, you don't look at the rightness, the justness, you look at the law that was in effect at the time they entered the treaty, and then you have to construe that, so that the right continues up until today. So, they created this concoction called the Doctrine of Discovery, John Marshall made it a part of the legal system of the United States, that's the law at the time, so to interpret those treaties and laws now, you have to say under this Doctrine that if it was valid then, its valid now. And brothers and sisters, this is a struggle that is going on in the world today. Indigenous people all over the world are going before the United Nations to claim the right to their indigenous territory. They are asking the European countries, they are asking the United Nations, to void the Doctrine of Discovery, to rule it illegal and unlawful because on the basis of this Doctrine, their lands have been taken, their families have been destroyed, their civilizations have been destroyed. Just as recently as May (2012), I think there was a meeting of the United Nations Permanent Forum on Indigenous Issues, in Brazil, where they discussed the Doctrine of Discovery, and that's why I thought it was important brothers and sisters to bring it before you because until I started doing this research, I did not have a clue about it. This is going on in the world, all around us and we are sitting here in darkness. Our slave Master will not teach us about this. You're not going to find it, you can have as many advanced degrees as you like, you are not going to hear it. But it is an ongoing struggle in the world today, asking for the repudiation of the Doctrine of Discovery. So, this brings us brothers and sisters to the new Age of Discovery. Because while they are asking that the Doctrine of Discovery be repudiated, personally I don't have a problem with it. I don't' have a problem with it at all, because there has been a new discovery. And the New Doctrine of Discovery is in full effect. So, the Bible says your covenant with death shall be disannul and your agreement with hell shall not stand. See the scriptures are telling us that something else is going to happen, that is going to void all this stuff they are doing and then the Holy Qur'an Sura 67 said "Blessed is He in Whose Hand is the Kingdom and He is Possessor of Power over all Things". So, we are talking about a new discovery now and in Sura 3 25 & 26 says:

> "Say Oh Allah Owner of the kingdom, thou givest the kingdom to whom thou pleases and taketh away the kingdom from whom thou pleases and thou exalteth whom thou pleases and abases who thou pleases in

thine hand is the good. Surely, thou are possessor of power over all things. Thou maketh the night pass into the day and maketh the day pass into the night and thou bringeth forth the living from the dead and bringing forth the dead from the living and thou giveth substance. sustenance to whom thou pleases without measure."

So, brothers and sisters there has been a new discovery. See We believe that God appeared, Allah, God appeared in the person of Master W. Fard Muhammad, July 4, 1930, the long awaited Messiah of Christians, and Mahdi of the Muslims and we believe further that Allah is God and beside Him there is no God and he will bring about a universal government of peace where we may all live together. Right? So, this discovery has now taken place and the Honorable Elijah Muhammad says, in Message to The Black Man:

"Allah came to us from the holy city Mecca, Arabia in 1930 he used the name Wallace D. Fard and often signing it W.D. Fard and the third year 1933 he signed his name W. F. Muhammad which stands for Wallace Fard Muhammad. He came alone, he began teaching us of knowledge of ourselves of God and of the devil and of the measurement of the Earth and of the Planets and the civilization of the planets other than Earth. He measured and weighed the Earth and its water, the history of the moon, the history of the two nations, black and white, that dominate the Earth. He gave the exact birth of white race, the name of their God,

59

who made them and how in the end of their time the judgment and how it will begin and end. I asked him who are you, what is your real name, he said I am the one the world has been expecting for the past 2000 years. I said to him again what is your name, he said my name is Mahdi, I am God, I came to guide you into the right path."

So, Praise Allah, and under this Doctrine of Discovery, upon discovery what had to happen? There had to be a surveyor, so this God came and produced a survey, right? He gave us the total area of the land and the water, 1,963,940,000 square miles, brothers and sisters, after I did this research I began to look at this book, "The Supreme Wisdom" all together different. This is not just a teaching, this is a legal document. So, he conducted the survey and gave us a survey so that we would know what belongs to us. He gave us survey questions; Who is the Original Man? The Original Man is the Asiatic Black Man the maker, the owner, the cream of the planet Earth God of the universe. These are survey questions. See when you go and do the survey you have to say who's already there, describe the people. What's the land? What's the water? What's the Mountains? It's a survey. What's the population of the Original Nation in the wilderness of North America? You see it's a survey and he gave the survey answers. The population of the Original Nation in North America is 17,000,000 with the 2,000,000 Indians make it 19 million, all over the planet Earth 4,400,000,000; it's a legal document that's filed with the Lord of the World brothers and sisters. Then he gave us a flag. Every nation got to have a flag, is that right? We are not talking about a flag of blue with stars and red and white stripes. Elijah Muhammad taught us what that blue meant, its deception. It's an illusion. The red is the blood, that we shed, and the white is his domination. But we have a flag made of the Sun, the Moon and the Star. Everyday you wake up, you wake up under the Sun and you go to bed at night, and before you go to bed, you look up in the sky and you see the stars and the moon, it's the universe. What better flag could a man want? He gave us this flag.

Then he raised his Messenger to stake the claim for us. See somebody got to stake the claim. So, the Honorable Elijah Muhammad says, "we want our people in America whose parents or grandparents were descendants from slaves to be allowed to establish a separate state or territory, of their own. Either on this continent or elsewhere." He stakes the claim based on the lawful right, on the warrant that has been issued, on the survey that has been rendered. Now we got a claim to stake, anywhere on this planet is ours, see. People say well why don't you go back to Africa. We don't have to go nowhere. All of it belongs to the black man, so the Doctrine of Discovery in this new Age of Discovery applies to us. First there is a discovery, and Master Fard Muhammad found us and was the first to declare us a nation. And then there is actual occupancy, so we established temples and mosques and study groups all over this country. And now it's spreading all over the world. There is preemptive title, Who is going to deal with this white man about our condition? Farrakhan told us pool our resources, give it to him (through the Economic Blueprint) so he can buy land for all of us. Not just the church going and buying 20 acres and building some homes. Not just individuals getting a little cash and buying a couple acres and building a home. Who is thinking about the Nation? Who has the authority to deal for the Nation? To negotiate for the Nation? It's Farrakhan! Nobody else has the authority. They (our enemy) don't even respect anybody else enough to talk to them (about our independence) to deal on our behalf. Next Terra Nullius, if it's vacant, we claim it. So, at the Million Man March, the theme of it was from II Chronicles, "if my people who are called by my name will humble themselves, pray and seek my face and turn from their wicked ways, then I will hear from heaven, forgive their sins and heal their land." See, Christians, we say Islam, not in the narrow sense, but if you truly understand Christianity you've got Islam. You can't walk the walk of Jesus and not be a Muslim. You can't walk the walk of a Muslim and not be with Jesus. See they are one in the same but what was being taught was this made up white man's religion. It's a slave making religion, but the true

Christianity will set you free. Civilization. We are given in this legal document the requirements of civilization. What is the meaning of Civilization? One having knowledge, wisdom, understanding culture refinement, is not savage, seeking the pursuit of happiness. What is the duty of a civilized person? To teach the uncivilized person, who are savage righteousness the knowledge of himself, the science of everything in life, love, peace and happiness. And conquest; that was another part of this Doctrine of Discovery. So, we are told in this document that we have, how then Allah, would separate us from the Devils and then destroy them and change us into a new and perfect people and fill the Earth with freedom, justice and equality as it was filled with wickedness, making we, the poor lost found, the perfect rulers. So, the Honorable Louis Farrakhan, said in the Origin of Blackness Study Guide:

> "There is a new God with a new wisdom, he is the Original Man of a brand new, reality. That is why the question is asked who is and not Who was. See that Original Man that lived trillions of years ago, he is not here. There is a new Original Man being made right now in this class, that we are in, in this nation of Islam. The Original Man is a new black man, he is the maker, the owner, the cream of the planet Earth and if he stays in the class he will become a God of the Universe."

So, what are our Marching Orders Brothers and Sisters? What are we to do now? We have this new discovery, we have got the Doctrine, we have the wind behind our backs with the Doctrine of Discovery. What do we do? Do we go out and start picketing. Do we go out and buy guns and stage a revolution? No sir, that's not what we are asked to do. The Honorable Elijah Muhammad says,

> " I am not trying to get you to fight, that's not even necessary, our unity will win the battle. Not one of us, will have to raise a sword, not one gun will need to be fired. The great cannon that will be fired is our unity, our unity is the best. Why are you afraid to unite? Why are you afraid to accept Allah and Islam? Its only because the slave Master didn't teach you."

So, brothers and sisters what we are inviting you to, is a nation submissive to God. This is the nation that Abraham and Ishmael prayed for when they repaired the foundation of the Kaaba. So, the Honorable Elijah Muhammad tells us in his book, The Flag of Islam:

> " since our flag has been given to us to represent an independent nation, its referred to as the Flag of Islam. All this makes up the flag; all this makes up the flag of Islam which is the sphere of life in the whole universe of space and man. The nature of this sign, this is important, the nature of this sign is the greatness of the unlimited wisdom of the designer. The great source of goodness for all that is under and in the flag of Islam. The Freedom, the Justice, the Equality that is freely exercised by both believer and non-believer, under the flag of Islam. Which is revealed for the soul purpose of teaching the great unlimited source of mercy and love that the designer has for his creatures."

Now, take a look at our flag, it said freedom, justice, and equality for the believer and the non-believer. So, we are not talking about some exclusive cult here, we are talking about a real nation, that is all inclusive and will be governed by righteousness. So even the unbeliever can live in it, just got to follow the law. Just as the sun shines on the wicked and the righteous, they both get the benefit of Allah's mercy. The Honorable Minister Louis Farrakhan said that when Israel came out of Egypt, they were of mixed multitude, so this is not a racist teaching, it is a righteous teaching. It's not really about black against white, it's about good against evil, see. There is room in this nation for the Latino, the Indian, the Asian, and even the white, if we but submit to the law of righteousness. So the Honorable Louis Farrakhan said "is this just for blacks, are only blacks suffering, if just for our Latino family, is this just, for Asians, is it for whites, yes it is because when the children of Israel went out, it was a mixed multitude that went out. For those whites who want to come out from under this Satan's world, take the door, let us unite and build a better world. And that's what we are inviting you to today brothers and sisters. We're inviting you to come join on with us in this new nation to build a better world, don't we need a better world right now? On the tone scale, what's the lowest on the tone scale, apathy? Which is one step from death. Are we so apathetic that we don't want change in our lives? Well one has come he has found us. He has surveyed the land and given us our survey. He has given a legal document by which we know we are inheritors from the Lord of the worlds, from the creator who made all that is. So, all we have to do now brothers and sisters is unite, come and join on and build this new world. And with that brothers and sisters I close and I leave you, I have enjoyed myself. I leave you as I came before you in our nations greeting words of peace,

As Salaam Alaikum.

MANCHILD IN THE PROMISED LAND

In the Name of Allah the Beneficent, the Merciful, I bear witness there is no God but Allah, who came in the person of Master Fard Muhammad, to whom praise is due forever. I bear witness that the Most Honorable Elijah Muhammad is the Exalted Christ, and The Honorable Minister Louis Farrakhan is the divine reminder in our midst, and in their names, I greet you in our greeting words of peace, As Salaam Alaikum

"The Age of Discovery Part 2: "Manchild in the Promised Land". Let me give a little background on the title, "Manchild in the Promised Land ". I was on my way to the mosque, last Sunday, and while I was driving I started to think back to when I was in High School. I had two great English teachers. I went to M.C. Williams Senior High, in Acres Homes, and this was before integration. I had two teachers that taught me things that helped to sustain me to this very day, and I want to give them their props. One was Mr. Chester Smith, who taught me how to research and organize information, and write it, in terms of a research paper. I basically used what he taught me all through college and through law school, and through my practice of law. There was another teacher name Mrs. Evie Smith, and what Mrs. Smith did was show me how to read, and not only remember and understand, but to think creatively, on the basis of what I had read. So, she gave us a project where we had to choose a book, and read it and then produce something tangible, as a result of, what we had read in the book. So, the book I chose was "Manchild in the Promise Land", by Claude Brown.

MANCHILD IN THE PROMISED LAND

A MODERN CLASSIC OF THE BLACK EXPERIENCE

CLAUDE BROWN

"THE FIRST THING I EVER READ WHICH GAVE ME AN IDEA OF WHAT IT WOULD BE LIKE DAY BY DAY IF I'D GROWN UP IN HARLEM" — NORMAN MAILER

It was a very popular book in the 70s and 80s. I don't know how popular it is now, but it is a very well read book, and it was an autobiography of a young man who grew up in Harlem. It told the story of his life growing up in Harlem, the crime, the violence, the drugs, and how he was able, to rise above his conditions, and make of himself a better man. I read the book and for several days I didn't know what to do to produce something tangible. The night before our project had to be turned in, I had this idea. I got a birdcage and I got a doll, one my oldest sister had left in her closet, and pulled all the hair out of the doll. I got some shoe polish and painted this doll black and sat the doll inside of this birdcage. I got a cigarette and twisted it up to look like a marijuana joint and put an empty beer can inside the bird cage, and put it on a white poster board. On the outside of the birdcage I wrote "employment", "college", and good "home". I didn't know I was talking about luxury, good homes, money, friendship in all walks of life. I had this idea, so I put it all on the board, and I took it to class the next day, and I got an "A". She told me she was very impressed with it, but what that taught me was how to read and understand, and then think creatively and then produce something. I don't know how much this is being taught in the educational system today, but it is the kind of teaching we need, it's the kind of teaching that our young people need. It is not good enough, just to read and understand, it's not good enough just to go by rote memory. It's not good enough just to pass a TAAS Test, and graduate. Because if you cannot produce something tangible, on the basis of the knowledge and education that you're getting, then you still have nothing. You are still a consumer, you still don't produce anything. So, I just wanted to give my kudos to Mrs. Smith for showing me and giving me that project to encourage me to study and understand, and how to then begin to produce something.

So, the title today is "Manchild in the Promised Land". I want to look at a Sura from the Holy Qur'an, this is Sura 17:89, it reads "we have explained to man, in this Qur'an, every kind of similitude. Yet the greater part of man refuse to receive it, except with ingratitude." I was curious about this word similitude and so I looked it up in the dictionary and basically it is a counterpart, it's a double; a visible likeness; an image; an imaginative comparison; a correspondence in kind or quality; a point of comparison. As we go forward, Insha Allah, you will see use of the similitude in what we are going to show. We are going to start with "The Age of Discovery" and this is what we discussed in our last presentation. In 1452, Pope Nicholas the V issued what was called the Papal Bull. In Islam, we might call it a Fatwa. It's a ruling or a statement. So, to understand the connection between Christendom principles of discovery and the laws of the United States we need to begin by examining a Papal document, issued 40 years before Columbus' historic voyage. Pope Nicholas V issued to the King Alfonso V, of Portugal, the Bull Romans Pontifex, declaring war on all non-Christians throughout the world and specifically sanctioning, and promoting the conquest by colonization and exploitation of non-Christian nations and their territories. So, based on this Papal Bull, issued by the Pope, Portugal began to engage in the discovery of the African continent. They began to make voyages down the African coast and set, as we know in our lessons, a trading post. The purpose of it was conquest, and exploitation of the non-Christian nations. After that, Christopher Columbus, sailed on behalf of Spain. The Popes edict was such that, it basically divided the world in half, and he drew an imaginary line in the middle of the world from North to South, so that everything East of this line would belong to Portugal. Portugal had rights to Africa and India and all to the East and to the West would belong to Spain. Now, they did not know there was a new land over in the Atlantic so he was thinking of Asia. So, Christopher Columbus set out to go to India and Asia, and he sailed in 1492. You know the old story, what they told us in high school, in 1492 Christopher Columbus sailed the ocean blue. So, Columbus sailed pursuant to this same Papal Bull, in search of lands to conquer by conquest and exploitation. This became known as the concept of discovery. If you have seen any of the movies of Columbus, when he lands, they get on the boats and sail to the island and they come on shore and plant a flag, and he says something to the effect of, I claim this land, or this territory, on behalf of the King and Queen of Spain. So, there is a ritual that is used to claim the land of being discovered on behalf of the sovereign, the King and the Queen for which he sailed. So shortly after that, John Cabot, sailed on behalf of the British and discovered what would become North America. He went through the same ritual on behalf of the King and Queen of England, I discover this land and claim this land on their behalf. Because this was their mindset, based on this Papal Bull, that they had the right, they had God's right to claim these lands on behalf of the sovereign. So, that is kind of the backdrop of this Doctrine of Discovery.

Where I want to go now is to look at the mindset of the people who came to this new land. When those immigrants left Europe, and came to America, what were they thinking? What was their mindset? What did they think that they were doing? What were they coming to found? Our thesis is that they were coming to found the "New Israel". And make America God's New Israel. So, let's look at some of the words of the people that were coming. Ezra Stiles was the President of Yale University and made this statement, "Then the words of Moses, hitherto accomplished but in part". Now, he is making reference to the biblical chapter of Deuteronomy. He says,

> "Then the words of Moses, hitherto accomplished but in part, will be literally fulfilled, when this branch of the posterity of Abraham shall be nationally collected, and become a very distinguished and glorious

people under the Great Messiah the Prince of Peace. He will then make theme "high above all the nations which he hath made in praise, and in name, and in honor", and they shall become a "holy people unto the Lord" their God. I shall enlarge no further upon the primary sense of literal accomplishments, of this numerous other prophecies, respecting both Jew and Gentiles, in the latter day glory of the church. For I have assumed text only as introductory to a discourse upon welfare of God's American Israel and as allusively prophetic of the future prosperity and splendor of the United States."

So, this shows that when they came to this land, they had in their minds the establishment of God's New Israel. Jonathan Edwards said,

"there are several things that seem to me to argue, that the son of righteousness, the son of the new Heaven and new Earth, when he rises, come forth of his church, rejoicing as a strong man to run his race, having his going forth from the end of the Heaven, in the heat of it shall rise in the west. Contrary to the course of things in the old heavens and the Earth."

Here we see John Edwards, who was a pastor in the 1600s, speaking of the Son of Righteousness, rising in the west, a similitude. When we hear the Minister, and the Honorable Elijah Muhammad's Teachings, talking about the sun rising in the west, you see, we don't have to apologize for that. Because the initial people that came to this country saw the sun rising in the west. John

Winthrop, who was a Puritan and helped to establish Massachusetts, sailed from England and said "we shall be a city upon a hill, the eyes of all people are upon us". The Puritan, John Winthrop wrote, "The Puritan's who disembarked in 1620 believed that they were establishing The New Israel. Indeed, the whole colonial enterprise was believed to have been guided by God. God had opened this passage onto us Alexander Whitaker, preached from Virginia in 1613 and led us by the hand, unto his work. So, this Promised Land imagery, figured prominently, in the shaping of colonial English thought. There is a point we are going to get to, so just bear with me okay, we are going to get there. I'm kind of laying a base right now, about this New Israel. So, when John Winthrop sailed, he said we are establishing this city upon a hill, a New Jerusalem. The official history of the Seal of the United States, was published by the Department of State in 1909. Gallilard Hunt wrote that late in the afternoon in June of 1776, the Continental Congress resolved that, Mr. Benjamin Franklin, Mr. John Adams, and Mr. Thomas Jefferson, be a committee to prepare a device for a Seal of the United States of America. In the design proposed by the first committee the obverse face of the seal was the code of arms of six quarters, with the emblems of England, Scotland, Ireland, France, Germany, and Holland. The countries from which the new nation had been peopled. So, if you see in the image of the initial seal, what Ben Franklin, Thomas Jefferson, and John Adams put on the seal, was Moses parting the sea while Pharaoh and his soldiers drowned, as they sought to chase Moses as he was about to go into the Promised Land.

Now, Minister Farrakhan has told us this before, right? I have always wondered why would Moses? Why would Benjamin Franklin? Why would Thomas Jefferson and John Adams use the imagery of the children of Israel and Pharaoh pursuing them and drowning in the Red Sea? It didn't connect with me, I accepted it, I mean the Minister says it, we follow it. But we should take what he tells us and study it and research it, dig down into it, to enable our faith to be strengthened. When I look at this Seal of Pharaoh drowning, I understand now that I have seen the words of John Winthrop, and I have seen these other words of the Puritans, and the people who first came to America, that it was this Promised Land imagery. It was this New Israel that was being created in this American continent, that was foremost in their mind. So, it was apropos for him to use this as an image, because they saw in the King of England, that they saw Pharaoh. In George Washington who led his army to fight the King of England and establish this new nation, they saw Moses. This Promised Land imagery is there, it's prevalent. So, this is why, Benjamin Franklin, and Thomas Jefferson chose to use this as an image. Well that image was not accepted by Congress so they formed another committee and they came up with the image that we have today, for the Great Seal of the United States.

It is a pyramid. It contains a thirteen-step pyramid with 1776 in Roman Numerals at the base. The eye at the top is the Eye of Providence, with the Latin motto, "ANNUIT COEPTUS", in the sky. Meaning, it, the eye of providence, is favorable to our undertaking, for he favors our undertaking. And below the pyramid the scroll reads "Novus Ordo Seclorum" Latin for the new world order of the ages. I looked up providence, what does providence mean? Providence is when God conceived initially directing the universe in the affairs of humankind with wise Beneficence. A manifestation of divine care or direction, foresight, provision; provident care. So, they saw and put on this seal, that there is a relationship between the founding of America and God. They saw that the United States as being something that has been providently guided by God, himself. That it was God's providence that enabled them to come and successfully settle this land. So, there is like a covenant relationship that they see, between America and God. There is a book called "Pagans in the Promise Land", written by Steven T. Newcomb. He's of the Shawnee Lenape tribe. He is a Native American. And in his book, he talks about, what he calls "The Cognitive Theory", which means that people's thinking really derives from their bodies, and how we live. In this model, he looked at what were the people thinking when they conquered America. He proposed there were two models used in the taking and conquering of the land of American. One was the Conquer Them All, meaning he who conquers rules. So, by the Europeans landing in America, they began a conquest, to conquer, and based on a conquering, they ruled. We see this model, at work, all over the world today. In other words, "might makes right". He also put for the model, The Children of Israel, which means the people who came, saw this virgin land as the Promise Land and saw themselves as the children of Israel. So, if you go back to the Old Testament when God gave the land to the Children of Israel, when they left Egypt, the land of Canaan, it was populated, right, there were people there. When he said, I am giving you this land to conquest and make it your own, it will be your land and I will be your God. So, this is on the mindset of the people who came to America, this Promised Land model. So, on this basis then, they began to continue with discovery, to survey the land, to mark it off. But now that they claim it, they can start to issue titles to it. Thomas Jefferson sent an expedition to explore all the land to the Pacific coast. This is the Lewis and Clarke expedition that they tell us about in school. The purpose of this Lewis and Clarke expedition was not only to find out what was there but also to stake out the claim of the United States for its territory. As you can see by the map the United States was still, mostly along the Eastern seaboard. They sent Lewis and Clarke on this expedition and along the way they followed the rituals of discovery, as they went to claim this. And this Doctrine of Discovery later became law. It became the law of the land for the United States through the Supreme Court decision of Johnson v. McIntosh. The Supreme Court Justice John Marshall ruled in 1823 that the Supreme Court, in the celebrated case Johnson v. McIntosh, quietly adopted the Christian Doctrine of Discovery into United States law. Writing for a unanimous court, Chief Justice John Marshall observed that Christian European nations had assumed "ultimate dominion" over the lands of America during the Age of Discovery, and that upon "discovery" the Indians had lost "their rights to complete sovereignty, as independent nations, and only retained a right of "occupancy" in their lands. In other words, Indians nations were subject to the ultimate authority of the first nation of Christendom to claim possession of a give region of the Indians land. As we said before, just by showing up the European minds said that we now own the land. So, for those of you who have been here for the last 15-16 thousand years you not only have the right to occupy the land, but that right can be extinguished by the new sovereign. We see this model played out all over the world, so when they go to India, now they claim right to the land. When they go into Palestine, and set up a new nation, they say, we have the right to the land, your title has been compromised by this Doctrine of Discovery. And on the heels of this Doctrine of Discovery, and now they have a legal under pinning of it, they spread across the land, what they call the Manifest Destiny. In the Manifest Destiny, we talk about again the attitudes and mindsets. This is a mindset that it is God's providence that has given us this land, given us entitlement to it. Even to extinguish the people who are already on it. So, they spread all the way from the east coast all the way to the Pacific Ocean, thinking that this was God's manifested will. And that it was the white mans manifested destiny to conquer, to own, and to rule.

So, if we look back at, as we said the founding of America, and how they saw this as a relationship between this country and God, a covenant relationship, this New Israel and God, we have seen from that point all the way up to modern times that God has been called on blessing America. Just recently, when President Barack Obama won the election, and during his acceptance speech, at the end, what does he say? "And God Bless, the United States of America". If you go back to every inauguration, you will see the president always says that "and God Bless, the United States of America". Why do they call on God to bless the United States of America? What's in the mind? You see they are referring to this relationship between God and America. President John Kennedy, in his inauguration speech in 1961 said, "The world is very different now, if a man holds in his mortal hands the power to abolish all forms of human poverty, and all forms of human life, and yet the same revolutionary beliefs for which our forbearers fought, are still an issue around the globe. The belief that the rights of man come not from the generosity of the state, but from the hand of God." This is the President of the United States saying that the rights come not from the generosity of the state but from the hand of God. Yet when we talk about a theocracy, they tell us that we are anti-American. But when you look at it, that's what they are talking about, really a theocracy, in what has been termed the American Civil Religion. That's Kennedy's inauguration address.

This is a concept that has been around since the 60s. A sociologist by the name of Robert Bellah coined the term "American Civil Religion" in 1967 in his article, "Civil Religion in America". When you think about it, the religion of America is America. I'll say that again, the religion of America is America. American and its constitution allows for religious freedom. And it says that the government cannot do anything to establish religion so people are free to practice, Christianity, to practice Islam, Buddhism, whatever religion they choose to practice, and still be an American citizen. But you must still be beholding to Americanism itself. So, now when they talk about Islam, they talk about they need a moderate Islam that is consistent with the ideals and the program of America. The Christians, right are saying, we need to take this country back because this is the American way. So, this writer coined this term, American Civil Religion, because he says America has formed a religion of Americanism, which exists parallel to, side by side, with other religions. And the founding documents, The Declaration of Independence, The Constitution, these are scriptures of the American Civil Religion. The founding fathers, George Washington, Thomas Jefferson, these are the prophets of the American Civil Religion. Abraham Lincoln is the Jesus of the American Civil Religion, because of his moral fiber that held the Union together and so called freed the slaves, and things of that sort. These are iconic figures in the American Civil Religion. When I looked at this, I began to understand some things. I understood more clearly now, when Barack Obama was running for the office of President, they brought up the speech by Reverend Jeremiah Wright, where he says "No, not God bless America, God damn America." Barack Obama had to distance himself; he had to denounce that, because in the American Civil Religion, that is a heresy. You see my point? That is a heretical statement because in this civil religion, God does not damn America, God only blesses America. Because America is God's making, America is God's vehicle that he uses to advance his purpose in the world. This is the mythology that has been developed around America itself. In Genesis 17, what I wanted to point out here was, Abraham and God, and God said, "my covenant will be with you, you will be the father of many nations." This is the language that the founding fathers drew on to say that they are of the branch, you remember what I read a little while ago, that said this branch of Abraham's seed will found this New Israel, so they are saying they are a branch of Abraham's seed, because he would make many nations.

Before I go forward I want to talk about the summary of the Doctrine of Discovery. Now to summarize the Doctrine of Discovery first there had to be a discovery, actual occupancy and current possession, preemption, which means the Europeans now had title, native title, which means that the original inhabitants now no longer have complete title, they now only have a native title and right to occupy, the religion would be Christianity, they would spread civilization and conquest. So, the question becomes, if we look at the whole thesis we have been giving, that America is this New Israel, and

America has established a relationship between God and America. This didn't come to me until a couple of days ago, I had been reading this information and couldn't figure out where I was going with the information that I had. Until, it dawned on me what the Minister had said, about two years ago, in Atlanta, when he asked, "Who Are The Real Children of Israel". Who are the real children of Israel? And in my mind, often times, even though I know he is talking about us, my mind still keeps going back across the waters to the Middle East somewhere and to Egypt, this whole motif, this whole image, of the children of Israel. But now I realize, America, this is Israel. This is Israel. I saw it on YouTube just the other day, when Netanyahu met with President Barack Obama, , he said, "Iran says that you are the Great Satan and that we are the little Satan", He said, "well on this last part we can agree, because we are you and you are us". So, Israel here and Israel there are one in the same, and this is out of Netanyahu's mouth. So, if this is Israel, here in America, God's new Israel, they brought some "children" along with them. And if we look at Abraham's prophecy where he would be the father of many nations, there was another part to that prophecy. And the other part to that prophecy is that his seed would dwell in a land that is not their own for 400 years, and at the end of that time God would come to judge that nation. So, that's what God did. God came in the person of Master Fard Muhammad to America. My contention is that on the coming of Master Fard Muhammad, a New Doctrine of Discovery came into effect. We talked about the similitude; and we have seen it in the Doctrine of Discovery. Now we see a new method of it, because now we see that Master Fard Muhammad found us in what he said was the wilderness of North America. Why did he use the term wilderness? He came to a land that had highways, buildings, streets, people, but he called it a wilderness, because he was discovering something that had been covered up, an actual occupancy. So we established temples and mosques all over this country and preemption of title. So, now the real title has changed into this new nation, this new people. And on to this new the Doctrine of Discovery, which works in our favor, to our benefit. So, we covered this in the last lecture but I wanted to bring it back up to show, like we said before, when we look at our Supreme Wisdom, this is not just a book of teaching. This is a book of lessons, but it is also an authority from the sovereign, from the Supreme Being that grants authority and title.

The Holy Qur'an Chapter 36 says:

> "O man
> By the Qur'an, full of wisdom
> Surely, thou art one of the Messengers
> On a Right Way,
> A Revelation of the Mighty, the Merciful
> That thou mayeth warn a people whose
> fathers were not   warned so they are
> heedless"

Warn a people who had not had a warning. The black man and woman in America never had a warning. We were brought here from all over the world. The people of America, the people of America, had not had a warning, not just us, the people of America, had not had a warning. So, he says;

> "A Revelation that thou mayeth warn a
> people whose fathers were not warned

The word does prove true, most of them, so
they believed not
Surely, we have placed on their necks, chains
raising up to their chins, so they have their
heads raised aloft"

And who do we see in chains today? Come to the
courts any day of the week, and see us walking out with
chains. The Qur'an says, "and we have set a barrier
before them and a barrier behind them and so we have
covered them so that they see not ". The other morning,
right after prayer, I was reading this to one of my sons,
and I asked him what did he think about what we were
reading. He said, "Dad it sounds like a grave to me". A
barrier before them and a barrier behind them, we have
covered them. You know in a grave they cover you up,
and you can't see. So, they are talking about living
people that are in a grave, dead. Spiritually dead,
economically dead, educationally dead, they are talking
about our people right now, who are in the grave. So,
he says;

"It is alike to them whether I warn them, or
warn them not, they believe not".

Now how many of our people do we go to, with this
teaching, and they just won't believe. They are in the
grave of ignorance and refuse to believe. So, it says
alike to then whether I warn them or warn them they
will not believe, Now, check this out,

"Thou canst warn him only who follows the
Reminder and fears the Beneficent in secret"

83

Think about this, it says you can only warn who follows the Reminder and fears the Beneficent in secret. So, let's cut right to the chase brothers and sisters, we got to follow the Reminder. We've got to get our people to see the importance of following Farrakhan. He is the Reminder in our midst. Because if they do not follow Farrakhan, they will not see and the warning will not take root. So, we keep repeating the same mistakes over and over and over and over. Because we have not taken heed of the warning, and why, because we do not follow the man that God has put in our midst to open our eyes. Allah says "so, give him good new of forgiveness for them, and a generous reward". So, that those that follow the Reminder, who then heed the warning, there is forgiveness and a reward.

Allah says;

> "Surely, we give life to the dead and we write down that which descend before their footprints, and we record everything in a clear writing and send out to them the similitude."

That's that word again similitude.

> "Of the people of the town when apostles came to it. It says when we sent to them two and they rejected them both. Then we strengthen them with a third. So, they said surely, we listen to you."

When Master Fard Muhammad first came, he came as a prophet. He came as prophet W.D. Fard. He raised Elijah, the Messenger, and some accepted but most rejected. Even the Nation went astray, after he departed

84

they went in another direction, and walked away Elijah. But it says in the Holy Qur'an we sent them who they rejected, and we strengthened them with tᵢ third. And the third one they strengthened them with is Farrakhan, who stood up to rebuild the work of his father Elijah Muhammad. It has been Farrakhan who has strengthened us, that got us back on the path.

So, I saw this brothers and sisters, as so important, that we teach our people the value and necessity of following the Minister. There is a place in the Qur'an that says "don't say you believe because belief hasn't entered your heart, just submit". So, those who don't believe, don't worry, study, pray, because belief will come to you, but follow Farrakhan. Who else do we have, to follow? Who else speaks for the whole? Who else speaks for the conditions of the oppressed all over the world? Who else speaks of the conditions of the black man, the black woman, the red man, the read woman, all of our people, all over the world, Farrakhan. Who else would we follow? Would we follow some politician? Would we follow a pastor who has his own denomination but only sees for the interest of his own denomination? It's not necessary to believe, in order to follow. We can debate Islam versus Christianity, versus Buddhism, we've got time for that. But who is the man who is leading the charge for freedom, justice and equality, in this country today? It is Farrakhan. Who is the man that is taking steps to provide for us food, clothing, and shelter? It's Farrakhan. Let me read something else from this same Sura. I will skip over to Verse 19. Now there has been this conversation because now the reminder is there. The people start saying that you are just a man like us. They say, "Who are you Farrakhan", because they have been taught to look for something spooky. So, the Qur'an says," Your evil fortune is with you." They see in what this world is bringing, evil. Why? Because they don't want to give up their own evil ways. We don't want to give up our alcohol, and our dope, and our tobacco, and our gambling, and lasciviousness. So, the Reminder says your evil fortune is with you, that nay you are an extravagant people. People that don't produce anything, just spend our money on rims, and gold teeth, and chains, right. An extravagant people. We buy what we want and ignore what we need. The Holy Qur'an says, "And from a remote part of the city, came a man running and he said 'Oh my people follow the Apostle'. Follow him who asks of you no reward, they are on the right course." What does Farrakhan ask of you for himself? He goes to these colleges now speaking to our youth and doesn't charge an honorarium. He pays his own way to go there, to unleash them. What is he asking for, for himself? He's on the right course. So, this man runs and tells us to follow the apostles. Who asks nothing from you. How many pastors can say that? How many politicians can say that? Farrakhan is the man. And that's where I finally arrived at doing all this reading and all this study and all this research. It brought me all the way back home. Farrakhan is the man we have to follow. Plain and simple. He's the one that's going to get us across, and when he does, he is going to say look what God has done.

So, Manchild in the Promised Land, Why did I choose that title? Because we are in a country that says it has a relationship, a God relationship, between the United States of America and God. So, I say to America if it was God's providence that brought you here, if it was God's providence that made you successful in your undertaking, who is the God in this relationship? Does God only bless America or can God also judge America? I will accept the premise that America is the handy work of God, I will accept that premise. But in this New Israel of America there are a group of children here. And why do we call them children? Because any of you who have children, you know they don't produce anything. You provide for their needs. You provide food, clothing, and shelter for them, right, but they don't produce anything. So, in America we have been children, not producing anything for ourselves, but learning to produce for others. Not making even so much as a roll of toilet tissue for us. We are men and women in America, in the Promised Land yet we are a Manchild, in this Promised Land. So, it's time to be a Manchild no more. In the Bible, it says, "when I was a child I thought as a child, but now that I grew up I put away childish things". So, it is time for us, as a Manchild, or men-children, in the Promised Land, to put away childish things, and get behind the man that is leading the charge. Minister Farrakhan has asked us to raise some money, to buy farmland, so that we can produce for ourselves in this promised land. Not for himself, but for us. He's asked us to come together, to build our communities. I will read this from the Honorable Louis Farrakhan and then I will close.

He says,

> "I represent the Honorable Elijah Muhammad, a Messenger from All-Mighty God to black people, to America and the world. I do not speak to you from mere personal design but I speak in the name of the God who raised the Honorable Elijah Muhammad, and I am backed by them both. This statement that I just made should be given careful, study and weight, because whenever Warners or

Messengers appear this represents God's intervention into the affairs of that nation. Because in God's sight neither the people nor their affairs are in the right state. The gravity of the situation in God's own integrity demands his intervention to warn us of the consequences of our deeds that we may take a better course. This course of action demonstrates God's mercy and his desire to redeem over his right to punish, and destroy. In the case of the United States of America, God's warning must be sounded regardless to how painful it is and no matter what the consequences to the warner.

So, the Honorable Louis Farrakhan is the warner of America. He is that reminder to us. He is the one that is calling us to rise as a nation. To no longer be a Manchild in the promise land. To stand up to be men and women in this covenant with God. I agree with the founding fathers, that there is a special relationship between America and God. But we need to take it a step further and understand that God has now come to America, and that the judgment is now upon America. But it is incumbent up on us to stand up and be the people that God would have us to be. So, to that brothers and sisters I close, as I came before you in the greeting words of peace,

As Salaam Alaikum.

THE BURDEN OF DEBT

In the name of Allah the beneficent the Merciful I bear witness there is no God but Allah, who came in the person of Master Fard Muhammad. The long-awaited Messiah of the Christians, the Mahdi of the Muslims. Who came seeking and searching to find that which was lost. He found one man, one specially prepared man, born in Georgia, living in Detroit. He raised that one man and taught him, from himself, face to face. That one is the Most Honorable Elijah Muhammad, his Messenger, his Christ, who raised the Nation of Islam, here in the wilderness of North America. He (The Most Honorable Elijah Muhammad) found one man, and raised him and poured himself and the spirit of Master Fard Muhammad, into that man. That man being the Divine Reminder in our midst, the voice of God today, the Honorable Minister Louis Farrakhan. and it is in their names I greet you in our Nation's greeting words of peace, of As Salaam Alaikum.

The Honorable Elijah Muhammad taught us to say a particular prayer. He said that this prayer was specially designed for the black man and woman in North America. He encouraged us to say this prayer every day. It says, "Oh Allah, I seek thy refuge from anxiety and grief. I seek thy refuge from lack of strength, and laziness. I seek thy refuge from cowardliness and niggardliness. I seek thy refuge from the burden of debt and the oppression of man." This subject started in my mind, what I am about to present to you today, during the latter parts of the Presidential election (of 2008). As we saw the news of the economic crisis come to the forefront, as I watched that, and we subsequently saw our Brother, President Barak Obama, win the election, the economy was at the forefront, is that right. As I watch these developments, I started to ponder on this economic situation, and why we say the prayer seeking refuge from the burden of debt, and the oppression of man. I looked up the word "AND" in the dictionary and it is used to join elements of equal grammatical value. So, you have an element, and then you have the word "and" and then an element on the other side and they are of equal value. It is also used to show a consequence or a result. So, the thing, or the topic of my lecture today is, The Burden of Debt and the Oppression of Men.

What is the relationship between the burden of debt and the oppression of men, and why were we given this to seek refuge from? So, when we look at burden, what is a burden? The dictionary says that a burden is something that is carried, something that is emotionally difficult to bear; a source of great worry or stress; a weight. Oppression is an unjust or cruel exercise of authority or power. So, we are being taught that debt is a burden. It is something that is carried that causes great stress and worry, and oppression is a cruel exercise of authority. So, what is the relationship? What is the burden that debt carries? At some point in our lives we are all in debt. We all have to use resources in terms of goods, materials, even people. No man is an island, no man lives alone, is that right. So, we all become indebted in some form or fashion, but does that carry a burden? So, I submit to you that there is a particular burden that is carried, in relationship to debt, that we need to seek refuge from, and that burden is interest. Interest is something carried on top of debt, and I submit to you that that is what creates the burden. Now we are going to get into that.

To start with, what is a debt, and what is money? Interest is that which is carried to pay a debt, for money. What is money? Money is said to be anything that is generally accepted as payment for goods and services, and repayment of debts. The main usage of money is for a medium of exchange, a unit of account, and a store of value. To perform these functions, money must have certain characteristics. It must be available, it must be affordable, durable, fundable, portable and reliable. Generally speaking, it has fulfilled this criterion for thousands of years. Metals such as gold and silver, and sometimes bronze, were used as a monetary raw material. So, what is a debt, debt is that which is owed. A debt is created when a creditor lends a sum of money to a debtor, and in modern society, debt is usually granted with expected repayment, and in many cases plus interest. So, a short history of profit and money. In the development of money, we see in early civilizations, an exchange in society was whatever was needed or wanted. For example, I grew an orange tree and you have some corn, I like corn and you needed some oranges, so we traded oranges for corn or whatever was needed. Then when society developed into the age of empires, local forms of money was used as a vehicle of money, through which good were exchanged, sometimes this was salt. There was a point in time in which, the Arabs and the brothers of the northern part of Africa, traded salt for gold in West Africa, because they (the Arabs) had a scarcity of gold. The brothers in West Africa had gold mines, and they kept those gold mines hidden; they were a secret. They needed salt, so they had what was called a blind barter. The brothers would go to the gold mines and mine gold, and then the traders would come with loads of salt, and arrive at an agreed destination, and set an amount of salt out. They would then go back to their camps. The brothers would then come set out an amount of gold, and then go back to their camp. The traders would come back and look at the amount of gold against the amount of salt, and if they did not think it was a fair deal or an equivalent, they would go back to camp. The brothers would have to bring more gold, and they would go through this process until a deal was struck. This way the salt mines were protected and the gold mines were protected. So, because of the development of trade and the level of civilization, particularly in the Islamic world, trade demands money or compensation. So, the goal of society, which was less developed, and had less developed economic systems would tend to purchase more, which means that their gold would be delivered to the society that had full production. Over time, the Islamic world came to possess the majority of the gold in the world. Countries like Britain, France, and Europe, were suffering from a shortage of gold. There is only so much gold in the ground, only so much gold that was accessible, so to obtain gold, they either had to find it and dig it, or they had to obtain it through plunder. A little-known secret, and something that is seldom discussed, is that one of the major reasons for the Crusades, was not for the birth place or the burial site of Jesus, it was an act of war, for plundering of the Middle East or Islamic society, to get the gold back to Europe. Gold was a valuable commodity.

Eventually, paper money began to be used as currency. Profits were made on production and trade deficits became accessible. There was a young mathematician around 1202, his name was Leonardo of Pisa or he is also called Fibonacci. Fibonacci studied and published a book of calculations in 1202, in which he introduced to Europe the decimal system. What he actually studied, was the teachings of the Muslims; the wisdom of the Muslims, who had created the decimal system and the Arabic numbers. You can't do higher mathematics with stick figures. Roman numerals just wouldn't get it. Fibonacci studied the wisdom of our people, and published it in this book of calculations and he showed how it could be applied to commercial bookkeeping. The currency conversions were crucial to the calculations of interest. This is what led to the beginning of the banking industry. We are going to get into that. So, modern and post-modern, twentieth and twenty-first century, we see profit is made on capital, in which money is made on money. Having money makes you money. Now we see a rise and paramountcy of credit cards, checks, and sometimes you don't even have to have money in your pocket, you just show them the little plastic card. It's all debits and interest. Virtual money. I listened to the Honorable Minister Louis Farrakhan and he has taught on this. It was really an eye-opener for me to really dig deep into this, because I know I have heard the Minister talk about the Federal Reserve and the banking systems and the international bankers. I must admit some of what he said really went over my head. I heard it but it really did not get down into my being, but as I studied it, I gained another level of understanding of it. It became more real to me. Now, I go back and listen to those same lectures, or study those same lectures and they take on a whole new meaning and whole new significance.

The Medici family was a family of bankers, in Italy. They were one of the most powerful banking families in history. They perfected the art of banking, using Fibonacci's method of calculations to record transactions. What they realized was to be a more successful bank you had to be a bigger bank. So, they expanded the scope and operations of the bank, and became the most powerful family in Italy, to the extent that they actually controlled the Pope. They put one of their heirs on the Papal seat. I believe it was Cosimo de Medici became the Pope of the Catholic Church, because they were the power behind the throne.

In Amsterdam, the Amsterdam Exchange Bank of 1609 was another important development, because they solved the problem merchants had dealing in multiple currencies. Then, there was no unified or single currency, so merchants would sail into Amsterdam and they would have the currency of their locale, and wanted to enter into trade, so there was a problem of determining what is the value of your currency as opposed to my currency. So, the Amsterdam Exchange Bank solved that problem by allowing merchants to set up an account denominated in a standard currency. So, no matter what currency you had they found a way to value it and issue a receipt that would be common across the board. Now the interesting thing, and it wasn't discussed in the particular book where I got this information, was who the merchants were. What was the trade that stimulated this need for currency? Insurance and all of that as well. It was the slave trade, it was the trafficking of human cargo. They had to operate on such a massive scale that one single bank and one merchant would not suffice, so they had to form cooperatives in order to handle the economy and scale of the slave trade, they traded in other things as well, but the traffic of human bondage was the primary and motivating factor in this. Then the bank of England, in 1709, allowed the banks to operate on a joint stock basis, which means they allowed the banks to incorporate and sell shares of stock. This increased the revenue basis of the bank. As a result of that, certain banking families rose up.

Minister Farrakhan has taught us about these banking families. So, we see the Rothschilds were a family of German, Jewish, origin. Their prominence began with Mayer Amschel Rothschild, and his brilliant idea was to keep banking in the family. As Minister Farrakhan has taught us, he had five sons and he sent each son to a different country to establish a bank, and thereby ultimately gain control of the government through that bank. It is said that the Rothschilds financed both England and Napoleon Bonaparte in the same war, so it did not matter who won, as long as there was a war going on it made money. So, they profited off of war. The next family we see is the Rockefellers, now there were many other European banking families, the Warburgs, but I just wanted to give a sample. The Rothschilds were the most powerful banking dynasty in Europe, whereas, across the waters here in America, the Rockefellers held that position. They made the world largest private fortune in oil, through Standard Oil and through banking. They currently are known under the brand of Chase Manhattan Bank. That's a Rockefeller asset. The Rothschilds wanted to get a hold in America but they couldn't because the Rockefellers had staked it out. The thing is, that they still worked in consort. Another banking family, J.P. Morgan, has been stated to be one of the most influential bankers in history. So, what happed is the Rockefellers had the Manhattan Company and Morgan had Chase, so they actually merged The Chase Manhattan Corporation and J.P. Morgan Chase Bank and formed J.P. Morgan Chase Manhattan, working together to monopolize the industry. Now, the biggest banks in America is Citigroup, and Citigroup still belongs to the

Rockefellers, so we have Citigroup, Chase Manhattan and Bank of America. There was always a struggle between government and banking, going back to Alexander Hamilton and Thomas Jefferson, the founding fathers. There was always this debate as to who should have the authority to print money. Now, the Constitution gives the authority to coin money and determine the value of money, to the government. There were always the banking interests who always wanted to get the authority to be the ones who actually print money and control it. This went back and forth until finally in 1913, the Federal Reserve Act was passed. Of course, Minister Farrakhan has taught us in-depth not only on the Federal Reserve but also that, at the time the Federal Reserve Act was passed, the IRS was formed and the income tax was implemented, the FBI and the ADL. So, they had to circle the wagons, to pull this off. President Woodrow Wilson was duped in assisting in passing this Act, because they had tried to pass it before, it was called the Aldridge Bill. Senator Aldridge actually met with the bankers at a place called Jekyll Island where they came up with the plan to take control of nations banking systems. They called it the Aldridge Bill but it could not make its way through Congress, because during this time there was this lively debate as to what type of currency America would have. There was a strong movement called the Populous Movement, and their spokesperson was William Jennings-Bryant who ran for president. They were aware of what was going on, so they voted it down, but it came back as the Federal Reserve Act to make it look like it was federal, or appear as a government act. Right before Christmas while many of the Senators and Congressmen were out of town, they snuck the bill on the floor and they put it into Law. Wilson subsequently stated that, "I have unwittingly ruined my county".

What's so significant about the Federal Reserve having the authority to control the currency of the nation? This is going to take us back to where we started, talking about interest. It is because they control the method of creating money. First, the government, by Constitution, has the sole right to coin money and determine its value. They still have that sole right. So, we start off with the government needing money. So, how does the government get money? They issue what is called securities or treasuries, United States Treasuries, otherwise called bonds. Let's say they want to issue a stimulus package to the tune of $700 million dollars, they will actually issue $700 million in bonds, and a bond is nothing but an IOU. Its written on a piece of paper that says IOU $700 million dollars and they put the bond out for sale, through bond dealers. Bond dealers are special banks that have the exclusive right to go and obtain these bonds and sell them on the market. I can't just go say, give me $100 million of those to go sell, there is a special relationship between the government and these special banks to give them the authority to sell these bonds. They go out and sell these IOUs and institutional investors purchase these IOUs, foreign governments purchase these IOUs, pension plans, retirement plans, and also the Federal Reserve. Now, if a pension plan purchases a segment of those bonds, they are going to use money that is already in circulation. If the Fed purchases the bonds, this is where the trick comes in, because the Fed literally creates money out of thin air. The Fed sends a check to the U.S. on a piece of paper, well now they can do it through a computer entry, issuing, say, $700 million dollars to the U.S. government out of thin air. It is not

97

backed by anything, they don't have to go into a reserve and pull it out of existing money, they just create it by writing it down or putting it in a computer. Now, the Fed owns this bond, or this IOU but guess what, the nature of the bond says for this $700 million, the U.S. government will pay it back within 10 years, so that is attractive to the investor because they have the backing of the credit of the United States government guaranteeing payment in 10 years. Where the profit comes for the investor is not only will the U.S. pay it in 10 years, but will pay semi-annual interest payments on the bonds. This being the Federal Reserve, now owns the bond, they have received a guarantee the bond will be repaid, and now the government of the United States has to pay interest to the Federal Reserve. Where do they get the interest payments from? The income tax. They take it out of your and my paychecks before we ever see the money. The Federal Reserve owns treasuries, this is how when the Federal Reserve, when they want to expand money in the country, they buy the T-Bill or the Treasury Bond.

Next step, now the government has the money, the government spends the money. Public service projects such as the railways, bridges, whatever the case may be, when the government spends the money it trickles down into our hands. When it gets into our hands, we will just say the public, what do we do with it? Sooner or later we are going to go back to what, a bank and put it into our bank account. So, we are looking at money that has been created out of nothing, thin air, that now carries an interest payment to the owner of that bond. The trick continues, I'm talking about some real smoke and mirrors here. Once it goes into your bank account the banks then creates more money. So, it's a money-making machine. This is called fractional reserve banking. The Federal Reserve lists a requirement that the banks have to hold a certain amount of money in the reserve, that may be 10%. The bank can then loan out 90% based on the deposit that was just made. Let's say, person A deposits a $1000.00 government check into the bank. That goes into their account, because that goes in their deposit account, the bank can now create $900 of new money and loan that to person B to purchase a car. Person B buys a car, and I am sure most of you are familiar you go to a bank you fill out a loan application and they say you are approved. They loan you $10 thousand dollars. They don't give you $10 thousand dollars in cash, right, it just shows up in your bank account. It goes into the computer, customer A now has $10 thousand dollars in his bank account. Where does that money come from? They made it, they just put it down on a piece of paper and a computer and created it out of thin air. They had a reserve of $100 dollars still sitting there in the bank. Now, the bank did not have to go into that $100 or that $1000 dollars to loan $900. That $1000 stays on the books and they can loan it over and over and over, as long as they don't go into that 10% reserve. So, customer B buys the car and deposits $900 into bank number two. So, now bank number two can take that $900 and can loan 9 times that. Bank number two can now loan $810 in the form of loans to other people, and on and on and on. So, the banking industry actually creates money based on this fractional reserve.

Now how did the fractional reserve start? I found this very interesting. This really goes back to a time of the goldsmiths, when people were called goldsmiths. People would carry gold and silver around. They would go into a town for business or whatever and deposit their gold or silver with a goldsmith. The goldsmith generally had the best house and strongest safe and some men with swords or guns, or whatever to protect it. They would deposit their gold or silver with the goldsmith, and the goldsmith would issue them a certificate, that they could redeem for their gold, whenever they got ready to use it or leave. These stores of gold and silver began to accumulate in the hands of the goldsmith, and they would issue the certificates, and people began to just use the certificates. It was easier to exchange a certificate, saying hey I have 100 pounds of gold over at the goldsmith's place, and this certificate allows you to redeem $20 of it, directly from the goldsmith. This was easier than going back to the goldsmith and getting some gold and carrying it back around, and safer as well. So, as these certificates became more popular, the goldsmiths realized that at any given point in time, no more that 10-20% of the people who made a deposit, ever came back to get their gold. They began to issue certificates based on gold that was more than the gold that they were keeping. They realized that as long as they kept 10-20% of the gold in reserve, at any given point in time, they would only have to return 10-20%. They began to write certificates well in advance of the gold that they actually possessed in their storehouse. They only reserved a fraction of it for a time a person came to redeem it. That was the beginning of the fractional reserve banking. It's really based on a lie, because when they issue that certificate, that certificate would say this 100-pound certificate is redeemable in gold on demand. So, if everyone who had a certificate showed up at the same time, there would never be enough gold to pay the certificates. They hedged their bet, they were gambling on the fact that no more than 10-20% of the people would ever show up at any given point in time.

This developed into fractional reserve banking. Now, again this is based on a lie, cheating, right? It' robbing and exploitation. The goldsmith became extremely wealthy by playing with other people's money. There are some people who had a problem with that, and just didn't think it was right, because the rise of these bankers, made them want to control government. Even before the passage of the Federal Reserve Act there was always this banking interest in the country, I am talking about America. They were behind the seat of government pulling the levers.

There is a book I am going to discuss with you in a minute called, "The Web of Debt", by Ellen Hodgson Brown, who is an attorney and holds a Juris Doctorate. She says that the movie, "The Wizard of Oz", was written by a gentleman by the name of Frank Baum. "The Wizard of Oz" is really a metaphor for the banking industry and the economic crisis in America during that time. So, the man behind the curtain, pulling the levers, Oz himself was none other than the national bankers, using smoke and mirrors. Men all along have stood up to these bankers.

Minister Farrakhan talked about some of those people, Abraham Lincoln.

Abraham Lincoln wanted to prosecute the civil war and he knew it would take money so he was approached by the bankers that said they would finance his effort, because Britain was financing the south. They did not want to see a unified and strong country on the American continent. So, the bankers went to Lincoln and said they would finance the war, but they would charge him between 24-36% interest, and Lincoln refused to do it. He recognized that the government had the authority and the power to print and coin money, so Lincoln printed his own money, called Greenbacks. He put these green backs in circulation and financed the war efforts of the north, through using government issued currency, the Greenback. The beautiful thing about the Greenback was, since the government issued the Greenback, they did not owe it to anybody, so it carried no interest with it. It was debt free money. James Garfield, opposed the bankers. He said that "the preservation of public credit and the resumption of species payment so successfully attained by the administration of my predecessors have enabled our people to secure the blessings which the seasons have brought." Then he said whoever controls the money, in any country is absolute master of industry, legislation, and commerce.

President John F. Kennedy, opposed the bankers. Kennedy, upon taking office, was faced initially with the Cuban crisis. The Bay of Pigs, which was a big fiasco. That wasn't his idea, that was dropped in his lap. There was also a little war heating up over Vietnam. Kennedy did not see where that war was going to be beneficial to the interest of the American people, but he also understood banking and commerce. So, he had a problem with the Federal Reserve as well. He looked forward to ending and breaking the power of the Federal Reserve.

He issued the Executive Order 11110, in June of 1963, which authorized the treasury, the government, to issue treasury certificates backed in silver. So, he issued his own money, backed by something real, something solid. It was debt free because the government issued it. It was not borrowed money. Each of these men paid for it with their lives. Shortly after the Civil War was won, Lincoln was assassinated. James Garfield didn't last as president for four months, and he was assassinated. Of course, you know, Kennedy did not make it through his first term. Anyone who has come to stand against these international bankers, are walking in the valley of the shadow of death, because of their power and greed and wickedness.

I asked myself, as I continued to study, what does God say about this? We understand this is the system that we have, but what does God say about this? In Revelations, 18:1, it says, "Now came one of the seven angels, which had the seven vows and talked with me. Saying come hither and I will show unto the, the judgement of the great whore that siteth upon many waters, with whom the kings of the earth have committed fornication and the inhabitants of the earth have been made drunk with the wine of her fornication."

Now we know the kings of the earth, Minister Farrakhan taught on this. The word fornication is used.

Not marriage, but fornication. A relationship, that is not sanctified by an oath. In other words, they have an option to do other things such as globalization. What is that? In a literal since, it's the process of transformation of local or regional phenomenon into global ones, and be described as a process by which people of the world are unified into a single society and function together. This process is a combination of economic, technological, social, cultural, and political forces. Globalization takes place as a result of international monetary system. Now, just what is that? The international monetary system is a system in which international exchange rates are determined. Going back into the differences in currency. You have to establish a mechanism of evaluating currency. So, foreign exchange rates are determined, international trade and capital flows are accommodated and a balance of payment adjustments are made. There are institutional arrangements between countries that adopt or govern these exchange rates of currency. That's called the international monetary policy.

The history on the international monetary policy goes back to before World War I. In the late 1800s, the world policy was based on the gold standards and the power backing the gold standard was Britain. Britain was the number one colonizer in the world. It was in their interest to have a unified currency, so that wherever they opened up a colony, otherwise known as a market for trade, they would have stable currency. As a result, the gold flowed to Britain, so they backed the gold standard. Every country had to peg their currency against the value of gold. As I said, there is only so much gold that is above the ground. So, the country that has the benefit of a trade balance obtains the gold. So, if India is trading with Britain, and India produces cotton and other things, and they are trading with Britain but their currency, because of their lack of gold, their currency does not have sufficient power to be equal to what their trade balance is, then they have to ship gold to Britain. Think back to old western movies, there was always some group of guys hiding on the side of the trail or up in the mountain, waiting to highjack the stagecoach. It didn't click with me until I studied this. Why is the stagecoach carrying gold cross country? It's because there was a trade balance between a bank, for example, in San Francisco and one in St. Louis. When they had to settle their accounts, the bank that was in a deficit (San Francisco) had to literally and actually ship gold to St. Louis. That's why they had to get the stagecoach, and put the armed guards around them and, that is why the bandits laid in wait to highjack the stagecoach, to get the gold. There is an old saying that the British coined that, "he who has the gold rules". This gold standard was in operation but what they never disclosed was because of fractional reserve lending, there was never enough gold to cover the debts that were in circulation. It was still a shell game even though it was backed by gold. It was still based on a lie. Cheating people out of their hard-earned money. With the advent of World War I, Britain suffered devastating losses to their economy because Britain, at that time, was the banker to the world. They financed trade and production, development, all over the world, by creating debt, and getting paid interest. I'm currently reading a book, where they are talking about how Britain did not want to enter World War I because they had banking relationships with all of the countries in World War I, including Germany. So, they were saying they would face a devastating financial loss if they were pulled into the war. As a result of World War I, they suffered financially. So, after World War I, a group of bankers met in a place called Bretton Woods, and their objective was to recreate the financial world and reinstitute the gold standard. By now, because of war production, guess who had most of the gold? It was America. America sought to still proper Britain, so they backed the British sterling pound.

So, this is some history that leads to us to where we are today, because out of Bretton Woods came an institution called the International Monetary Fund. Now the International Monetary Fund, their primary mission was to regulate the exchange rates. They were to police monetary systems by insurance and maintenance of the fixed exchange rate and promote international cooperation, and facilitate growth of international trade. The real problem with the IMF was their relationship with developing countries. Countries where our people live. Countries in Latin America, in Asia and primarily in Africa. It is the International Monetary Fund that these countries would have to go to in order to settle their trade accounts. They are taking in aid and with aid comes debt, and with debt is interest payments. This is why, for 30 years Africa has been receiving billions of dollars in aid, yet their economies are still struggling. People are still starving to death. With aid comes debt, and interest payments that they can never meet. The International Monetary Fund comes in and tells them in order to meet our requirements you are going to have to make some structural changes in your country. Ron Paul, knows what's going on, and he didn't stay very long in the Presidential race either. Ron Paul says our whole economic system depends on continuing the current monetary arrangement, which means recycling the dollar, is crucial.

So, out of Bretton Woods another institution was created, which was called the World Bank. The World Bank's mission was to fund development in these Third World countries. These two institutions act together to police and manage world debt. The system that the IMF and World Bank was faced with was called conditionality, no reforms, no money. They would impose fiscal discipline, in other words, they would tell countries what kind of monetary policy they were going to have to operate on. They would reform the taxation in the country. They would liberalize interest rates. They would raise spending on health and education. The education was controlled by them. They would privatize state run industries and deregulate markets. They would adopt competitive exchange rates and remove barriers to trade and remove barriers to foreign investment. This is where the oppression comes in, because when they go into a country and remove trade barriers, when they remove barriers to foreign investments, that is when the bankers can come in with their corporate finance and move local production out of the way. So, now in countries where people are starving to death you have McDonalds and KFC on every corner. So, they can't stimulate their own productive forces in their own countries. In the name of globalism, in the name of free trade barriers, in the name of foreign investment.

There is another aspect of this banking crisis, or this banking industry that I want to discuss and that is called derivatives. A derivative is the trade and bank instruments or securities which are derived from the underlying assets. Let's take the example of your mortgage, you go and buy a home and get a mortgage. The mortgage company bundles those mortgages and then sells them to Fannie Mae or Freddie Mac or third party investor for a discount. That investor is entitled to the stream of income from not only this mortgage but hundreds of mortgages which have been bundled together. So, that is a security now that is derived from these individual mortgages. Then it goes further, because that holder of that asset can create another security, which is what we call strips. So, they may take the principle and then strip the interest payments, bundle the interest payments and create a security out of interest payments only and then sell that. Now, it's three stages removed from the underlying asset. That person gets these interest payments bundles those and then sells those to a pension fund, to insurance companies, you even have banks now dealing on their own accounts. The banking industry has evolved to where they are no longer just lending money, and financing your loan, they actually trading in their own account and they are buying these derived assets. These derivatives have now matriculated all over the world. Everybody has now invested in these derivatives, so now poor Joe Blow falls on hard times, and loses his job, the wife gets sick and they can't make their mortgage payment. Who owns the mortgage now? There used to be a time a person could to the corner and talk to the local banker and say "Mr. Joseph you have known me for all these years, you know I'm going to make good on my loan. I have a crop coming in, I just opened up a mechanic shop, I'm going to make good on it." As he owns the mortgage, he could say "I have you know you for 20 years, I know your wife and your children, you can stay in the house and we will work something out." Now, the owner of these mortgages, are divorced from the owner of the homes. So, who is foreclosing on these mortgages, but more importantly, what ripple effect takes place when these underlying assets starts to default? That's what you see now in this crash that they (the news) are talking about. These derivatives have flooded the market and the underlying asset is jeopardized by default because of the state of employment, now, these banks and these holders of these investment securities are insecure. They are calling in to the person that sold to them, to make good on it. It's kind of like a bank run. It's similar to everyone showing up at the goldsmith saying that I want my gold, at the same time. It's similar to everyone showing up at the bank saying I want my $1000 and the money is not there. The underlying asset is not there. So, in 2008 we saw the recession cause the industrialized world, to crash. They call it an economic downturn, but it is a crash. It's a crash because it is not based on anything tangible and real. You can't go and collect what was put out. So, now we see a G20 Summit Meeting, where these twenty countries went to London, to try to confer, not at the root of civilization, but to confer at the root of the devil's world, to see what they could do about this economic crisis.

The G20 is made up of 19 countries, Argentina, Australia, Brazil, Canada, China, France, Germany, India, Indonesia, Italy, Japan, Mexico, Russia, Saudi Arabia, South Africa, South Korea, Turkey, United Kingdom and the United States and then also the European Union. The Union is represented by a counsel of presidency and the European Central Bank. So, the European Central Bank is sitting at the meeting of the G20 and not only that, the managing director of the International Monetary Fund, the president of the World Bank, and the people who attend these meeting are the finance ministers and the heads of the central banks. It is they who are at risk in this crash, because they floated these derivatives and backing these governments and are sucking wealth from the world through these interest payments. So, they have to come up with a plan, and the plan that they came up with was that the G20 would give $1.1 trillion dollars to fight the global crisis. Now, I am not an economist, but it just seems to me, that this seems kind of funny. They have acknowledged that the economy has crashed, they have acknowledged that their governments are bankrupt, yet they pledge $1.1 trillion dollars. Where is the money going to come from? You have central banks and the governments of these countries that are going to issue bonds, create debt, attach interest to it, and create the money out of thin air. They are going to create the money out of thin air, and here is the trick, they say they are going to use the $1.1 trillion dollars to make it available to developing countries. President Obama went also to try to persuade them to also do a stimulus package, so at least the people in the countries can get something. He was trying to say, he knows what's going on, but he is saying if you are going to run the game at least the people need to get something. They shot that down, they said we don't need anything to stimulate our economies, but we are going to give a trillion dollars in made up money, monopoly money, to developing countries so we can put them deeper in debt, and extract the wealth of their countries through interest payments.

So, again as I get to my conclusion, what does God say about this? In Exodus, 22:25, it reads, "if you lend money to any of my people with you who is poor, you shall not be like the money lender to him. You shall not exact interest from him." Deuteronomy, 22:19, "you shall not charge interest on loans to your brother, interest on money, interest on food, interest on anything that is lent, for interest." In Leviticus, it reads, "if your brother becomes poor and cannot maintain, himself with you, you shall support him as though he were a stranger and a soldier and he shall live with you, take no interest from him, or profit."

What did Jesus say about it? When Jesus went into Jerusalem, he went into the temple and in Matthew, 21:12, 13, it says, "Jesus went into the temple and drove out all who were buying and selling there. He overturned the tables of the money changers and the benches of those selling doves. It is written he says to them "My house will be called a house of prayer but you are making it into a den of robbers." Who were the money lenders? What were they doing in the house of God? They were exchanging currency to the visitors and the travelers who came to Jerusalem, and profiting off of the exchange rates. They were loaning money adding interest in the house of God, and Jesus went in and drove them out. He whooped their behinds and ran them up out of there. Like the Minister said, "where are these preachers that say they follow Jesus." Who call Jesus' name all day and all night, but won't speak upon the truth. What does the Holy Q'uran say about it? The Holy Q'uran says in the Al-Baqara, "those who eat Riba or Usury or interest will not stand on the day of resurrection except like the standing of a person beaten by Satan, leading him to insanity. That is because they say trading is only like Riba, Allah has permitted trading and forbidden Riba or Usury. So, whoever receives an admonition from the Lord for Usury or interest shall not be punished for the past. His case is for Allah to judge but whoever returns to Usury, such as the dwellers of the fire, shall abide their end. It says Allah shall destroy Usury and give increase to deeds of charity. It says oh you who believe, be afraid of Allah give up what remain due to you from interest, Riba, from now onward if you are really believers. There is a Hadith that I found, it is by Hazrat Abu Huraira it says, "it is reported that a prophet said a time will come over the people when none will remain who will not devour Usury, if he does not devour it, its vapor will overtake him." That means it would become a worldwide problem. Now let's look at the conflict to see if the seeds of conflict in the world are based on monetary policy. See it's the money behind the situation that causes people to fight. They'll use the name of religion or democracy, but its monetary policy.

Monetary Conflict
and the Seeds of War

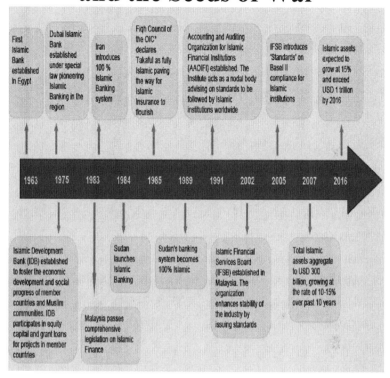

Now, I want you to look at who you see on the news as the number one enemy of America, Iran. They have this big problem with Iran. In 1983, Iran introduced a 100% Islamic banking system, which means in their Constitution, they outlawed interest. They developed a banking system devoid of interest, they developed financial products, based on some type of equity and justice, and just balance, devoid of interest. So, that means that the international bankers cannot penetrate their country, to exploit them and their people. The Sudan, we hear all about the Sudan, and Darfur and it is terrible that people are dying and starving, but the Sudan launched Islamic banking in 1984. We see the development of financial institutions, Islamic based, financial institutions. The Cold War, between America and Russia, was between competing economic systems. With the fall of the Soviet Union, and the demise of the Cold War, who became enemy number one? Islam. What does America have against fundamental Islam? Is it because our women, our sisters, dress in modesty? Is it because we call on Allah? Is it because we strive to pray five times a day? Or is it because the fundamentals of Islam will kill and destroy their economic system?

All we have to do brothers and sisters is be Muslims, be Muslims. The Honorable Elijah Muhammad told us about the fall of the dollar. He said the fall of the dollar would be the number one fall. In Iran, Mahmoud Ahmadinejad the (then) president said at a meeting, that the fall of the value of the dollar was one of the biggest problems facing the world today. The damage caused by this has already affected the global economy particularly of those of energy exporting countries. What did they do? The Minister said this, I heard it but it didn't hit me until I looked into it. Minister Farrakhan told us, that Iran had set up an oil bourse, I didn't know what a bourse was, so it really didn't have an impact. A bourse is a stock market. Iran set up a stock market where they would get away from depending on the dollar and begin to peg their oil revenues on other currencies, on the Euros, and a basket of currencies. It is by them going away from pegging against the dollar, which more and more countries are going for, that is accelerating the fall of the dollar, and creating for them an enemy in America. In Islam, the concept of Riba, means that there is no interest on money. This really needs two lectures because there is so much history behind all of this.

The development of Islamic finance and banking is relatively new because of the destruction and fall of the Ottoman Empire and colonization by European countries, but it is a force that is now rising. It is a force that is against Western financial imperialism. Interest free cooperative society, interest free cooperative housing society, cooperative investment funds, and Islamic bankers. I submit brothers and sisters that these are the kinds of things that we have to look at now in striving to be Muslims. God told us to come out of here and how can we come out of here if we are still entangled in their web of debt. We can never escape, so we have to look at ways among ourselves to create businesses and relationships, financial relationships based on the fundamental teachings of Islam. You might say well what does this have to do with the teachings of the Honorable Elijah Muhammad? This all sounds good and maybe that orthodox Islam. Where did the messenger talk about this? Where is this in our Lessons? Well in Supreme Wisdom, Lesson 34, "the uncle or Mr. Fard lives in the wilderness of North America and works 16 hours out of 24 every day for very little pay. He has a large family to support and on top of that a Satan came along and sold him a life insurance policy and gave him a written guarantee that he will receive full benefit at once, after the approval of his death." Gave him a life insurance with a guarantee after death. It kind of sounds like a religion I heard of too. We have a brother that is working 16 hours a day, that's a double shift, and he has a large family and is making very little pay. He goes and buys a life insurance that is only good, after he dies. Who sold it to him? Not a devil but a Satan, a wicked one. Whose evil is not only confined to himself but affects others. This Satan comes along and sells this poor man life insurance. Then on top of that, another Satan comes along and sells him 500 B shares at 6% in the Panama Canal at $1.75 per share. B shares are not a high grade of stock, B shares have conditions on it. You may not be able to vote, you may be second in line when it's time to get your dividends, in other words you may have just bought nothing. So, a Satan comes along and sells him 500 shares. This lesson was given in 1930, 500 shares at $1.75 is about $900. How far would $900 have gone in 1930, that is a lot of money for a man who is working 16 hours a day, for very little pay, with a large family, who can hardly make ends meet. Further along it says, the Panama Canal was completed in 1914, at the cost of $375 million dollars. Mostly the biggest part of the sum belongs to the shareholders who we call the 85%. So, the 10% is extracting wealth from the 85%. Creating debt among the 85% with interest attached. This poor brother, they ask us to calculate how much water would he own. If we do the calculations what we find is that a black man in Detroit who is working a double shift, with a large family, has just spent $900 hard-earned dollars to own some water 1500 miles away in the Panama Canal. What we are being taught here brothers and sisters is to be wise in our financial decisions. Not to get tricked by the Satan, and find ourselves entangled in his web of debt. The question is asked can you fool a Muslim now days? Actually, you can, if he doesn't study. If he doesn't listen to the guide we have in our midst today. You can fool him every day of the week. If he doesn't take the words of the Honorable Louis Farrakhan, and then go into them and dig and find out their meaning. The Minister told us to take his lectures and parse them. Go into them and find the kernels of truth that lies within them. If we don't do that we can be fooled. Wise financial decisions. Disentangling ourselves from the devil's web of debt.

So, we seek refuge from the burden of debt and the oppression of men. Then we ask Allah to suffice us with that which is lawful, that we may refrain from that which is prohibited and make us not to want that which is beside him. Brothers and sisters thank you all for listening I leave you as I came before you in Nation's greeting words of peace,

As Salaam Alaikum.

COMER BY NIGHT GOD'S PLAN FOR OUR SALVATION

Bismilah ir Rahman ir Rahim. In the name of Allah, the Beneficent, the Merciful. I bear witness that there is no God but Allah, who came in the person of Master Fard Muhammad. And I bear witness that the Most Hon. Elijah Muhammad is the Exalted Christ and that the Hon. Louis Farrakhan is the Divine Reminder in our midst. And in their names, I greet you in our Nation's greeting words of peace, As-Salaam Alaikum.

Our subject today is, *The Comer By Night: God's Plan For Our Salvation.*

> "The black man must know the truth. To know the truth of the presence of the God of truth and that His presence is the salvation of the lost and found people of America is to know your life and its happiness."

Thus, said the Messenger of Allah, the Christ, the Most Hon. Elijah Muhammad. In his book, *Our Saviour Has Arrived,* this is the first sentence in the first chapter of the book. Because you and I must know the truth and it is the knowledge of this truth that gives us life. In the Bible, Jesus said to know the truth and the truth will what: set you free. But we must ask the question, what truth? Implicit in that statement is that we are not free, that we are a people in a state of captivity. Our freedom has been denied. Our ability to do for self has been denied. Our ability to determine our own future as a people has been denied. We are in need of freedom. So, he said to know the truth, the truth will set you free. Well, what truth will set you free? There are many facts that we could say are truth. I can say, "Brothers and sisters, today the sun is shining, it is not raining. That is a true statement. Is it not? Is that the truth that will set you free? I can say, "Brothers and sisters, I have on a linen black suit". That's a true statement, is it not? But is that the truth that is pertinent and relevant to our condition that will set us free. We must have a truth that addresses our condition. And if it is outside of the relevance of our condition, then it is a truth that is not germane and relevant to setting us free. So, what is that truth that will set us free? It is the knowledge of God in reality. It is the knowledge of the devil in his person. It is the knowledge of who we are, the time we live in and what must be done. That truth addresses our condition and will enable us to set ourselves in Heaven at once. We need a Saviour. So, our subject again is from Surah 86, *Al Tariq: The Comer By Night* which starts,

> "In the name of Allah, the Beneficent, the Merciful. By the heaven and the comer by night and what will make Thee know what the comer by night is. The star of piercing brightness." And then further on in the Surah it says, "Surely they plan a plan and I plan a plan."

So, we see here that one will come by night as a star of piercing brightness. What does a star of piercing brightness do? It brings us light. We are a people who are deaf, dumb and blind. I went to the dictionary to look up these words. Blind is lacking intellectual light; unable or unwilling to judge rationally; without regard to rational discrimination, guidance or restriction. So, we're not talking about a blind where your physical eye is inoperative, where it cannot perceive. We're talking about a spiritual blindness, a mental blindness, a lack of intellectual light. Deaf - having a sense of hearing that is inadequate, for the purpose of daily living; to hear with your ears and still not perceive or understand. Jesus said often in the Bible, "Those who have ears, let them hear". He was not speaking to the deaf and the mute. He was speaking to people who were talking back to him. They posed questions to him. How could they talk back to him if their physical ears could not perceive sound? But their spiritual ear could not perceive sound; unwilling to hear or to listen; not to be persuaded as to facts, argument, or exhortation. And that's many of us. We can hear the truth but we are unwilling to listen. No matter what I say to you, no matter what Min. Robert Muhammad says to you, no matter what the Hon. Louis Farrakhan says to you, you are unwilling to listen. You will not be persuaded by argument, fact or exhortation. No matter how much you are preached to. Min. Farrakhan said he is tired of preaching because you won't listen, unwilling. The Hon. Elijah Muhammad said it, "Stiff necked, hard hearted and rebellious". Regardless of how plain we make this teaching. Dumb – destitute of the power of speech; lacking perception or understanding; characterized by stupidity; having little or no meaning. So, any people who fits these characteristics; deaf, dumb and blind, suffer from a condition most appropriately termed as dead. And what we need is light. So, I looked up light – something that makes vision possible; spiritual illumination that is a divine attribute or the embodiment of divine truth; ultimate truth; something that gives life or individuality to a person; a vital spark. So, we who have been living here in the wilderness of North America are people that were captured and brought to this country as slaves as chattel property made to do the work of another to build their country, denied the facility of reading and of knowledge and education, robbed of our language, our culture, our religion and our God, placed in a dark place which is America, where their purpose was to cut off from us all avenues of light. We are in need of a Saviour. One who would bring a light to us, a piercing brightness that would be that vital spark that would regenerate us and make us stand up and come to life. And surely, they plan a plan and God said, "And I plan a plan". So, what we're looking at is a struggle here. We have a struggle between the wicked, the unrighteous, the devil who enslaved us and wishes to keep us in slavery forever. He has a plan to keep us down under the heel of his foot, to use us as a tool and a slave. In Revelations 12 it says,

> "And there appeared a great wonder in the heaven a woman clothed with the sun and the moon under her feet and upon her head a crown of twelve stars. And she, being with child cried, travailing in birth and pained to be delivered."

This woman bringing birth to this child is the woman bringing birth to our deliverer, is bringing birth to a new nation that would be an abode or an ark for us in these times of trouble.

> "...And there appeared another wonder in heaven and behold a great red dragon having seven heads and ten horns and seven crowns on his heads. And his tail drew a third part of

the stars in heaven and did cast into the earth. And the dragon stood before the woman which was ready to be delivered for to devour her child as soon as it was born. And she brought forth a man-child who was to rule all nations with a rod of iron. And her child was caught up into God and to His throne." (Revelations 12:3)

So now we see one who is bringing forth a deliverer, one to come for us and for our salvation. And we see the opponent, the dragon, the devil, the beast, the white man standing to devour this child at his birth to prevent the rise of one who would come to us and bring us the light, to prevent one from coming to us to bring us back truth that would set us free. This is the devil's plan but God has a plan! And God planned. In the Problem Book, Problem No. 32, it reads, "One of the conference members by the name of Mr. Osman Sharrief, said to the eleven members of the conference, the lost found Nation of Islam will not return to their original land unless they first have a thorough knowledge of their own. So, they sent a Messenger to them of their own." Now for those of you who are not familiar with this, this comes from the revelation which has been brought to us here in the wilderness of North America. We call it the Supreme Wisdom. These are the lessons brought to us by Master Fard Muhammad to give us a knowledge of our condition and the keys to our salvation in a mathematical language because there is no error in mathematics. One plus one is two and one plus one is two, is that right? There is no deviation in that. There is no grey area in that. So, the devil has planned to prevent the rise of our deliverer and God has planned. The devil is waiting for this child to be born and the conference members, the wise men who have observed our condition say that we would not return unless we first have a thorough knowledge of our own, unless we have a knowledge of that truth that will set us free. So, they sent a Messenger to them of their own. Now, this is all contained in your Bible and in the Qur'an. It's all right here. In Thessalonians 5:1, "But brethren of the times and moments you need not that I write to you for ye yourselves know diligently that the day of the Lord shall come as a thief in the night." You see because you have a struggle here. There are two plans in operation. There is a plan for destruction and there's a plan for salvation. So as Bro. Eric says, God operates according to a pattern, and if we read His scripture and if we are prayerful and eating right and dutiful, we can discern His pattern so that we will not be fooled today. Because Barack Obama is not part of the pattern, you see, but he is part of the plan. God has a pattern by which He will frustrate and defeat the plans of our open enemy. So, how will He get this deliverer in among us? How can this child be born when the dragon is sitting right in front of the woman looking right at her, waiting for this child to be brought forth so that he can devour the child? What is God's plan? So, He says in Matthew 24:27, "For as the lightening cometh out of the East and shineth even unto the West, so shall also the coming of the Son of Man be. Therefore, keep watch because you do not know what day your Lord will come." But understand this, if the owner of the house had known at what time of night the thief was coming he would have kept watch and would not have let his house be broken into. Who among us has a home, an abode, a residence knowing a thief is coming would not sit and wait. You'd load up your shot gun and sit right by the window and say, "Let that sucker come on in here, I got something for him." If you knew when he was coming you would prepare, you would plan and prevent him from entering. He would have kept watch and would not have let his house be broken into. It's like a man that has a beautiful daughter. He wants to protect her from those young hoodlums and thugs out there. So, he watches her, am I right? She's getting ready to walk out of the house and has a skirt up to here and he says, "Girl where are you going dressed like that?" He tells her brothers, "Who is she talking to? Who is she conversing with at school?" He keeps a watch on her because she is valuable. "...So, you must also be ready." Now that's you and me. This is a message for you and I. ".... You must also be ready because the Son of Man will come at an hour when you do not expect him". Now we've seen examples of this in our scripture. Pharaoh and Moses. Is everybody alright? We're not gone be long today but we're gone be strong. Those of you who know me, I don't come to preach, I come to prove a point and we're going to make it clear so that if you don't understand this, you are still deaf, dumb and blind. Pharaoh and Moses in Exodus, now you all know the background of the story of Moses, right? There's the Children of Israel in captivity in the land of Egypt, well you and I know that that's actually talking about us, right? But for now, for the time being, we'll go back to the story in Egypt and the king of Egypt. Well, before this, Pharaoh had observed the growth of the children of Israel in their land and how numerous they had become and he said, "We must deal wisely with them lest there come a war and they join on with the enemy and overcome us." So, Pharaoh devised a plan and the king of Egypt spake to the Hebrew midwives of which the name of one was Shiporah and the name of the other was Puah. And he said, "When ye do the office of a midwife to the Hebrew women and see them upon the stools, if it be a son, then ye shall kill him. But if it be a daughter then she shall live." I was reading in Ebony magazine this morning about the college campuses, how two thirds of the population on our college campuses today, particularly the black colleges, are women. There's an imbalance. The women are getting educated and the men are in the prisons or dropped out, abandoning education, abandoning the pursuit of knowledge. Our sons are being killed today. But the midwives feared God and did not as the king of Egypt commanded them, but saved the men-children. So further down in Exodus, Pharaoh realized what was happening because the birthrate of the males continued to rise. So, Pharaoh commanded all his people saying, "Every son who is born, ye shall cast into the river and every daughter ye shall save alive." Kill them! Slay them! So, it should not surprise you when you see the condition of our youth today, when you see the murder rate and the death rate among young black men. As Public Enemy had their logo, he's a target, right across his chest and on his back. And everywhere he goes they have him in their sights to kill him mentally, spiritually, emotionally, psychologically and yes, physically. But we know in the story of Moses that God had a plan. So, Moses' mother placed him in a basket and hid him in the bull rushes. And he floated down the river and Pharaoh's own daughter found him. And then one of the handmaidens went to her and said, "There is a maiden, a Hebrew, who would give him suck and nurse him." So, in God's wonderful plan, Moses survived. Not only did he survive, he was nursed by his own mother. And they plan and God plans and God is the best of planners. Herod and Jesus – the same pattern. They are looking for a deliverer. The Jews had studied the histories and prophecies. They were looking for a Messiah. And in this story a child was born and a star appeared in the heavens. And three wise men saw the star and Herod counseled with them. He said, "When you find Him come back and report to me, tell me who it is that you find. I would like to know." And these wise men traveled by the path of this star and found the baby Jesus. But they perceived what was in Herod's heart. They perceived Herod's plan and did not go back to Herod immediately. So, in Matthew 16 says, "The Herod, when he saw that he was mocked of the wise men, he was exceedingly wrought, angry, and sent forth and slew all the children that were in Bethlehem from two years old and under, according to the time which he had diligently inquired of the wise me." Again, kill the babies. Kill the young men so that a deliverer would not be born. It's like the terminator. You all have seen *The Terminator*, Arnold Schwarzenegger, what has happened? The machines have taken over, but one has risen among the humans, among the people and organized a rebellion and they are about to win, they are about to defeat the machines. So, they say, "We'll send one back in time to prevent this Saviour from being born." So, he goes back to find the mother, the woman bearing this child, to devour that child, to kill that child before he's born. They're showing it to you right on your television screen, right in your theaters. If you're deaf, dumb and blind you'll think it's only a movie. But if the light has come to you, you see God's pattern, you see His plan. So, God had a plan. He knew that they sought to kill the baby Jesus. So, he sent an angel to Joseph and said, "Arise, take Mary and the child and go into Egypt and stay there until he that seeks to slay you is dead." And then when Herod was dead, "behold an angel of the Lord appeareth in a dream to Joseph in Egypt saying arise and take the young child and his mother and go into the land of Israel for they are dead which sought the young child's life." And they plan and God plans. And God is the best planner. So that brings us to you and I because we know that we have been a captive here in this country and we need a Saviour. In churches, as I speak today, in churches across this nation people are praying for salvation. They either say that they are saved or trying to be saved. So, it's universally acknowledged that we need a Saviour. So, I'm here to tell you today, brothers and sisters, that our Saviour has arrived. All praise to Allah! On July 4, 1930, the long-awaited Saviour of the black man and woman, Master W. Fard Muhammad appeared in this city that is Detroit.

He announced and preached that God is one and it is now time for blacks to return to the religion of their ancestors, Islam. Now, many of you will say, "Well I'm a Christian. I'm a Buddhist." If you understand Islam, if you come into an understanding in reality, of what Islam is, you will understand that despite the title or the label that you wear, you are in fact a Muslim. Because a Muslim is one who submits. So, if you carry the label, Muslim, but you do not submit then you are not that which you profess. If you carry the label Christian but you're not living a Christ like life, then you say what you do not. If you say you're a Buddhist, but yet, you do not seek enlightenment, then you say what you do not. But if you are humble in your spirit, if you are submissive to the truth when you hear it, if you are submissive to God's plan when you see it regardless of what you call yourself, you are a Muslim and your religion is your nature, which is Islam. He says in the Qur'an, "This day I have perfected for you your religion and given you Islam as a religion, the nature of which you were created." So, Islam is not your religion, it's given to us as a religion, as a guide as a tool to help us to understand our nature and get into submission with our nature, which is made to be in accordance with the will and plan of God. And when we reach that point then we don't practice a religion, we live our lives naturally and our religion becomes our way of life. So, He gives us Islam as a religion. It's like someone who needs a purse to carry some goods in. But they don't have a purse, they have all of these items. So, someone comes to them and says, "I don't have a purse but here's a bag and you can use it as a purse". Well, the purse, the bag is not really a purse but it's being used as a purse to fulfill the function of a purse. So, Islam is given to us as a religion to guide us into our nature. Y'all with me? So, news spread all over the city of Detroit of the preachings of this great man from the East. Elijah Poole's wife first learned of the temple of Islam and wanted to attend to see what the commotion was all about, but instead her husband advised her that he would go and see for himself. That's a man. I don't know what's out there. I don't know who these people are. I don't know what you might be getting yourself into. You stay in the safety of our home and I will go. He's not going to expose his woman to just anything. And she submitted. You've got some women today that say, "I don't need you to go for me. I can go by myself. I can go here myself." And you got some men, you don't care where the woman goes or what she does. The Hon. Elijah Muhammad had it right from the beginning. He said, "I will go and see for myself." Hence, in 1931, after hearing his first lecture at the Temple of Islam, Elijah Poole was overwhelmed by the message and immediately accepted it. Immediately accepted it, he didn't prevaricate. He was not dumb. He was not deaf. He was not unwilling to listen. He was not one who would not be persuaded by argument or fact. When he saw the truth, and heard the truth, he accepted it immediately. Soon thereafter, invited and convinced his entire family to accept the religion of Islam. And we see this as a pattern also. The same with Prophet Muhammad ibn Abdullah (PBUH). When he accepted, when he joined, his wife joined with him. She joined with him in his mission and his work to help him meet his duties to their Lord. Mr. Muhammad quickly became an integral part of the temple of Islam. For the next three and one half years, Mr. Muhammad was personally taught by his teacher nonstop. In 1934, Master W. Fard Muhammad left without leaving a trace. So, at that point, the Hon. Elijah Muhammad took over leadership. After assuming leadership of the temple of Islam by the order, by the order of the family of the Nation of Islam, Mister Muhammad faced a death plot at the hands of a few disgruntled members. Mister Muhammad avoided their evil plan and went to Washington D.C. to study and build a Mosque there. He was known under many names, Mr. Evans (his wife's maiden name), Gulam Bogans, Muhammad Rasoul, Elijah Kareem, and Muhammad of U street. Consequently, Mister Muhammad, while in Washington D.C. was arrested on May 8, 1942 for allegedly evading the draft. When the call was made for all males between 18 and 44, this is the Hon. Elijah Muhammad speaking, "I refused, not evaded, I refused, on the grounds that first, I was a Muslim and would not take part in war especially not on the side with the infidels." He wrote this in the Message to the Black Man. "Second, I was 45 years of age and not, according to the law, required to register." So, now the Hon. Elijah Muhammad is on the radar. We have to put this in context; the United States is at war. It's a world war, they are drafting people to go into the military and here is this man, Elijah Muhammad on the streets of Washington D.C. with temples in Washington D.C. and Detroit and Chicago teaching them to accept their own. Teaching people that we are the original people and that we have our own nation and that the laws of Islam are superior to any man-made law. This man is dangerous now because the government wants young people especially black people in their military. As they do right now, so they arrested him. And now he is on the FBI radar, you may have difficulty reading this. But, this slide comes from the files of the FBI, so the next several slides will be directly from the files of the FBI to let you see what they see.

See many of you don't believe though your own open
enemy believes. You don't want to except the relevance
of Master Fard Muhammad, but your open enemy
understands who he is. Your open enemy understands
who Elijah Muhammad is, and who the Honorable Louis
Farrakhan, and what affect these teachings can have on
your lives and my life. And how it can raise up a nation
of freedom, justice, and equality for us. So sometimes
its good to look at your enemy, the Honorable Elijah
Muhammad told us to study him. So, at the time that
Gulam Bogans was arrested on 5/8/42, he advised that
he first meet Allah in 1931. And that this person went
by the name of W.D Fard, he stated that W.D Fard had
been arrested in Detroit on three different occasions for
teaching Islam. And that Fard was removed from Detroit
by the authorities on May 26,1933, he claimed that he
received all of his information concerning the Nation of

Islam and the Muslim set from Fard. He didn't go to college; he didn't go to the schools and the Madrasas of Islam. He learned it from Fard Muhammad, so it says by teletype dated 5/11/42 the Detroit office was requested to check the records of the Detroit police department as to W.D. Fard, and furnish any available criminal record and photograph as well as any information concerning Fard's whereabouts. Who is this man? Why is this man? I have a people that I have been guarding and I've been looking, on the look out, for that deliverer so that I may slay him before he comes to raise them up. Where is this man that has given his students theses teachings. When Elijah Muhammad was arrested on 9/20/42, a search was conducted at his home, 6026 S. Vernon Ave. Chicago. The following were among the numerous exhibits seized at that time.

Then Elijah Mohammed was arrested on 9/20/42, a
search was conducted at his home, 6026 S. Vernon Ave., Chicago.
The following were among the numerous exhibits seized at that
time:

No. 34-
Typewritten copy of publication, "The Final Call to Islam," Volume 1, No. 1, dated 8/11/34, at Detroit. Pages 1 and 2 contained these quoted remarks: "So they sent a messenger, in the person of Prophet Fard Mohammed, to teach us of our own, this is being done.".......The only way that Prophet Fard, can make us believe that he is our Deliverer, is to first show us how utterly ignorant we are of ourselves and how vain the worship of any God beside Allah."
(Remarks set out in further detail)

No. 57-
Handwritten minutes of Islam Temple meeting in Chicago on 2/3/35 reflecting the following statement by Elijah Mohammed: "You had better get unto your own kind. If you join onto the devil you will be the loser. The Asiatic Nation has the Ezekiel wheel ready to destroy this devil in 6 hrs. time. They are just waiting to hear the name of the Prophet W. D. Fard Mohammed."

No. 147-
Several copies of a pamphlet entitled "This book teaches the Lost Found Nation of Islam. A thorough knowledge of our miserable state of condition in a mathematical way, when we were found by our saviour W. D. Fard."

No. 158-
Two typewritten pages containing instructions given by W. D. Fard for laborers of Islam.

No. 176-
Steel cut on wooden frame. Print of steel cut reflected a picture of Prophet Fard addressing a congregation.＊

No. 177-
Pen and ink sketch entitled "Calling the Four Winds" which was a picture of a US map containing a figure in the center identified as Fard. Guns, bearing the name Asia on the barrels, pointed to the US from each side. The drawing bore the signature of R. Sharrieff.＊＊

＊ Alleged speech set out

＊＊ Islam Temple member

Number 34, (I hate that you can't see this) a type written copy of a publication, The Final Call to Islam. The Final Call. Min. Farrakhan, brothers and sisters, does not deviate. He does not and has not changed the teachings one dot or one iota. He went back to the root. Volume 1,

No. 1 dated 8/11/34 at Detroit. Brothers and sisters, when I found these slides, I nearly could not contain myself to read, this is a contemporaneous recording of what was happening. This is a close up look at what was happening as it happened.

So now, the FBI has arrested the Hon. Elijah Muhammad. They have his books. They have the Supreme Wisdom. They are reading this, which to a deaf, dumb, and blind people represents light. It represents that vital star that can bring to light. So now they go into action. They realize a thief has come under a cover of darkness. They missed him. They were looking for him but they did not see him. There are many people who have a problem with the complexion of Master Fard Muhammad, you see, because He looks like a white man. I've heard it said that one of the sons of Elijah Muhammad said that, "If had told me that you were Allah, I could accept it. But I have a problem with a white man, of a man who looks like a white man." But see, God had a plan so He slipped in among them 'unobserved' coming in sinful flesh to judge sin in the flesh. A Master plan, a wonderful plan! They knew he was in Detroit teaching. They knew he had raised twenty-five thousand. They arrested him three times, but they didn't know that he had pulled one close to him, put him under his wings, and taught him personally that which he had not taught everyone else. And then he left in 1934. And I will show you that he left without a trace and that devil was angry. So, we have a Federal Bureau of Investigation. This is a report made at Detroit, Michigan, date made August 6, 1942 for the period covering May 15, 16, 28th, 6/10, 11,12/42.

FEDERAL BUREAU OF INVESTIGATION

This case originated at WASHINGTON, D. C.   DETROIT File No. 100-5549

Report made at	Date made	Period	Made by
DETROIT, MICHIGAN	8/6/42	5/15,16,28; 6/10,11,12/42	████████

Title	Character
OULAN BOGANS, with aliases, et al.	SEDITION SELECTIVE SERVICE

SYNOPSIS:

Islam Group, Detroit, founded in 1931 by W. D. FARAD, known as WALLACE DON FARD, W. D. FARD, and ALLAH, who left Detroit in 1934, present address unknown. He has FBI No. 56062. Records indicate group has membership of approximately 700 in 1934, but meetings presently average from 30 to 35. Regulations provide for captains, secretaries, investigators, ministers, student ministers, teachers and treasurers, but not so organized at Detroit. Teachings are about freedom, justice and equality. No member is allowed to smoke, drink, attend movies or carry any sort of weapon. No member allowed to fight under any circumstances and so members refuse to register under the Selective Service Act. One member of Detroit group registered but is presently unclassified. Members claim registration for Selective Service not discussed at meetings. Printed teachings and problems studied by the group indicate the white man as the devil and that the law of Allah is supreme to any man-made law. No indication of Japanese influence in Detroit.

So, the report was made, for a period of time, prior to his arrest. So, what does that tell us? It tells us that the agents were already in, among us. The informants were taking back reports as they are today. See, many of you don't believe when we tell you that there are those who have come in, among us, and wear a white gown and a headdress and a black suit and a bow tie and then go back to their Masters to give a report. You don't believe it when we tell you this. But he is telling you himself. All praise to Allah! So, February 9, 1943, this is a slide from the Federal Bureau of Investigations, United States Department of Justice to the director, or from the director of the Federal Bureau of Investigations regarding Allah Temple of Islam, the Sedition Internal Security and Selective Service Act, "Dear Sir, it is requested that a wanted noticed be placed in the file of the identification division against the record of the following individual, name: Wallace D. Fard; alias W.D. Fard, Allah".

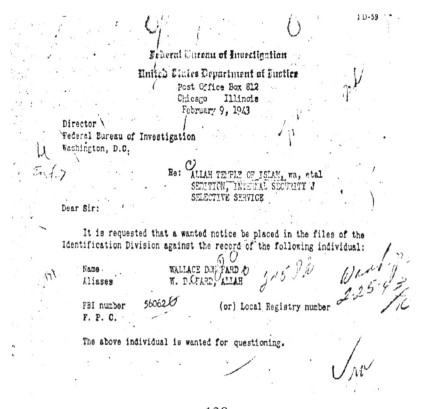

They called Him by His proper title, Allah! You don't want to accept Him as Allah, but your enemy calls Him Allah. "The above individual is wanted for questioning". They want to find Him. So, they searched all over for Him. They put all of their offices on alert, look for Him, search your records, find this man! We've got to stop this movement! We missed Him. He got into our niggers. Now we've got to stop this! They're in danger of being free.

"In 1957, subject W.D, Fard, reference to the San Francisco letter to the Bureau of 8/27/57, "For information of the Honolulu, Portland and Washington field officers". Washington D.C., Portland, Oregon, Honolulu, Hawaii, they are looking all over for Him.

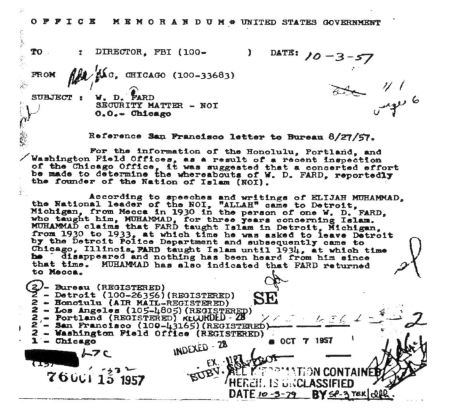

OFFICE MEMORANDUM • UNITED STATES GOVERNMENT

TO : DIRECTOR, FBI (100-) DATE: 10-3-57

FROM SAC, CHICAGO (100-33683)

SUBJECT : W. D. FARD
SECURITY MATTER - NOI
O.O.- Chicago

Reference San Francisco letter to Bureau 8/27/57.

For the information of the Honolulu, Portland, and Washington Field Offices, as a result of a recent inspection of the Chicago Office, it was suggested that a concerted effort be made to determine the whereabouts of W. D. FARD, reportedly the founder of the Nation of Islam (NOI).

According to speeches and writings of ELIJAH MUHAMMAD, the National leader of the NOI, "ALLAH" came to Detroit, Michigan, from Mecca in 1930 in the person of one W. D. FARD, who taught him, MUHAMMAD, for three years concerning Islam. MUHAMMAD claims that FARD taught Islam in Detroit, Michigan, from 1930 to 1933, at which time he was asked to leave Detroit by the Detroit Police Department and subsequently came to Chicago, Illinois. FARD taught Islam until 1934, at which time he disappeared and nothing has been heard from him since that time. MUHAMMAD has also indicated that FARD returned to Mecca.

2 - Bureau (REGISTERED)
2 - Detroit (100-26356)(REGISTERED)
2 - Honolulu (AIR MAIL-REGISTERED)
2 - Los Angeles (105-4805)(REGISTERED)
2 - Portland (REGISTERED) RECORDED - 28
2 - San Francisco (100-43165)(REGISTERED)
2 - Washington Field Office (REGISTERED)
1 - Chicago

INDEXED - 28

OCT 7 1957

76 OCT 15 1957

ALL INFORMATION CONTAINED HEREIN IS UNCLASSIFIED DATE 10-3-79 BY SP-3 TGK

139

"As a result of a recent inspection of the Chicago office, it was suggested that a concerted effort be made to determine the whereabouts of W.D. Fard, reportedly the founder of the Nation of Islam. According to speeches and writing of Elijah Muhammad, the national leader of the NOI, Allah came to Detroit, Michigan from Mecca in 1930 in the person of one W.D. Fard who taught him, Muhammad, for three years concerning Islam. Muhammad claims that Fard taught Islam in Detroit, Michigan from 1930 to 1933 at which time he was asked to leave Detroit by the Detroit Police Department and subsequently came to Chicago, Illinois. Fard taught Islam until 1934 at which time He disappeared and nothing has been heard from Him since that time. Muhammad also indicated that Fard returned to Mecca". This is from your enemy's files.

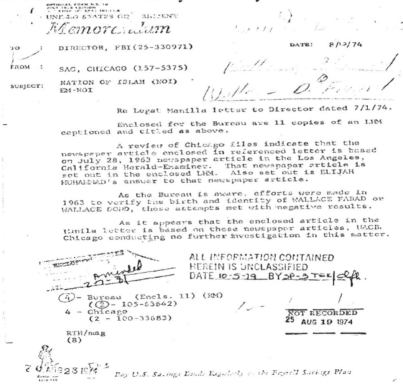

140

Dated August 12, 1974 (I'll only read part of it) A review of (now this, again, is from the United States government. It's a memorandum from the Chicago office) "A review of the Chicago files indicate that the newspaper article enclosed in a reference letter is based on a July 20, 1963 article in the Los Angeles, California Herald Examiner. The newspaper article is set forth in the enclosed LHM. Also, sent out is Elijah Muhammad's answer to that newspaper article." What had happened, they missed Him, they couldn't find Him so their next strategy was to discredit Him. They said, "If we can show that Fard Muhammad is a fraud, we will make the Nation of Islam and Elijah Muhammad appear ridiculous". So, they started on a campaign of propaganda. They released, through one of their organs, an article in the newspaper claiming in bold headlines, "W Fard Muhammad is a fake. He's a white man posing as a Negro." The Hon. Elijah Muhammad addressed it and said, "If you can prove it, if Wallace Dodd, is Master Fard Muhammad bring him to me and I will give you $100,000.00. Bring Him to me. Have him set in front of me and tell me that he is the one that taught me for 3 ½ years." "As the bureau is aware, efforts were made in 1963 to verify the birth and identity of Wallace Fard or Wallace Dodd. These attempts met with negative results. As it appears that the enclosed article in the Manila letter is based on these newspaper articles, Chicago is conducting no further investigation in this matter." All praise to Allah! (Let me move quickly) It's not over, see because they still seek to destroy.

So now we get…I wish you could see the picture. This is a picture of J. Edgar Hoover. And Psalm tells us about them. It says the wicked lie in wait for the

141

righteous seeking their very lives. Now, you can see even going back into the 40s that the FBI has been active, seeking to deny us a Saviour, to deny us a deliverer till now, they have missed Him and that which they feared has happened. They now seek to attack the Nation itself. So, in a letter expanding the program in the late 60s or the mid-60s rather, they expanded their operation and they had five long-range goals for the program. Number 1, to prevent the coalition of militant Black Nationalist which might be the first step toward real Mau Mau in America. Some of you don't know what a Mau Mau is. See, cause in East Africa, in Kenya when they were under the colonial yoke of the British the Mau Mau were the brothers and sisters that struck for their freedom. They attacked their enemy. They slew their enemy wherever they could find them. That's what the Mau Mau was. They don't want a Mau Mau here in America. To prevent the rise of a Messiah. A messiah for us, imagine that. Not a Messiah who loves everybody. Not a blond, blue eyed Jesus, stringy haired Jesus who teaches us to turn the other cheek and to love your enemy. A Messiah for the Black man and woman who can unify and electrify the movement. Meaning, specifically, Martin Luther King, Stokely Carmichael and Elijah Muhammad. To prevent violence on the part of Black Nationalist groups by pin-pointing potential troublemakers and neutralizing them before they exercise their potential for violence. To prevent groups and leaders from gaining respectability by discrediting them to the responsible Negro community, to the white community, both responsible community and liberals. The distinction is the bureaus. So, the bureau has distinguished, they've already told us who is who. You have the responsible Negro community, and then you have the liberal white community. So, they seek to discredit the leaders of the natural aspirations for freedom, justice and equality of our people from these responsible Negroes. The doctors, the lawyers, the educators, the politicians, they seek to distance them from the natural leadership that arises from our people. To prevent the long-range growth of these organizations, especially among the youth by developing specific tactics to prevent these groups from recruiting young people. This is the strategy of your open enemy. To prevent us from recruiting young people. The youth are the lifeblood of any movement, of any organization. This body, this will only house the spirit of God for so long, then I got to go. But if I can't get him and him to come in and pick up the torch we will die. So, our lifeblood is in our youth. Now, consider this. And there are those sitting in here who know this. Brother K. Rino knows this. In the beginning of hip-hop, the voice was that of Islam, of Muslims, of 5%. They talked about Allah and the lessons. Am I right brother? Many young people came to the Nation of Islam. They first heard the name Louis Farrakhan from Chuck D and Public Enemy. What happened? How did we go from Chuck D to Eminem? How did we come from a music that was the voice of the downtrodden, the CNN of the Ghetto, to a music that's all about hoochie mommas and pimps? How did we go from brothers who wore medallions with a fist on it to walking around with their pants showing their draws? What happened? Are these brothers on the pay roll of the FBI? I'm not saying that. Don't get it twisted, don't get me wrong! But, I've been a lawyer for 25 years; I've worked in the entertainment field for 25 years. I have seen record labels deny record deals to brothers like this brother. Stand up Brother K-Rino (Killa Rhymes Intellectually Nullifies Opponents). Y'all need to recognize this brother. This is one of the most talented artists in this country, who speaks truth and relevance to his people and can't find a budget. (A different brother from audience speaks that was not initially recognized) Stand up brother. This brother is a legend in his own time, here in the city of Houston. You should hear what he has to say. Yet he goes, these brothers go through all kinds of obstacles. You see, but Nelly can get millions of dollars for the tip drill. So, they don't have to have these brothers on the pay roll, they trick them. Like Min. Farrakhan said about O.J., we get pulled in. So, they get pulled in by the allocation of budgets and resources and marketing and promotions and control of radio. So, our youth are distracted now, so that they can't join on. We've got opposers brothers and sisters. Now the next slide is from 1967. You wont be able to read it of course. I'm going to read this to you and I'm going to move quickly.

"The purpose of this counter intelligence endeavor is to expose, disrupt, misdirect, discredit or otherwise neutralize the activities of Black Nationalist, hate type organizations and groupings, their leadership, spokesman, membership and supports and to counter their propensity for violence and civil disorder. (I'm going to the bottom of it) Emphasis should be given to extremist who direct their activities, and politics of revolutionary or militant groups such as Stokely Carmichael, H. Rap Brown, Elijah Muhammad and Maxwell Stanford."

See, you didn't believe when we told you that the FBI had been working against the Nation for all of these years. Many of you thought Min. Farrakhan was just paranoid or seeking fame and glory. But this is their documents. Now this is very important, it's leading up to our conclusion. This is dated January 7, 1969.

> "The direct of the FBI counter intelligence program – Black Nationalists, hate groups, racial intelligence Nation of Islam". The Nation of Islam does not presently advocate violence by its members, the group does preach hatred of the white race and racial separatism. The membership of the NOI is organized and poses a real racial threat. The NOI is responsible for the largest Black Nationalist newspaper which has been used by other Black extremist". The largest newspaper that's used by other organizations because they know it delivers the word of truth.

Check this out,

> "The NOI appears to be the personal fiefdom of Elijah Muhammad. When he dies, a power struggle can be expected and the NOI could change direction. We should be prepared for this eventuality. We should plan how to change the philosophy of the NOI to one of strictly religious and self improvement orientation deleting race hatred and the separate nationhood aspects."

What your enemy hates is that which is good for you! So, he wants to facilitate a change in the direction of the Nation away from nationhood.

> "In this connection, Chicago should consider what counter intelligence actions might be needed now or at the time of Elijah Muhammad's death

to bring about such a change in NOI philosophy. Important considerations should include the identity, strengths and weaknesses of any contenders for NOI leadership."

There's a name there. There are some names there. Informants in regards to leadership. They have informants who have penetrated the ranks of the Nation who may via for leadership. "How could potential leaders be turned or neutralized? The alternative to changing the philosophy of the Nation of Islam is the destruction of the organization." So, either they've got to change, they gotta stop calling the white man the devil. They got to step away from nationhood or we have to destroy their organization. And after the departure of the Hon. Elijah Muhammad the philosophy of the Nation did change. Master Fard Muhammad was no longer to be talked of. We were told He was not Allah in person. He was not our Saviour. We were told that the Hon. Elijah Muhammad was a good man, a social reformer but not the Messenger of Allah. The books of the Hon. Elijah Muhammad were taken out of print. You could not find them. You could not find Message to the Black Man, Our Saviour Has Arrived, Fall of America. We forgot How to Eat to Live. But there was one thing that they couldn't calculate on. Because you see, they had a plan, but God had a plan and the Hon. Louis Farrakhan disrupted their plan. Because after the departure of the Hon. Elijah Muhammad in 1975 and the assumption of leadership by Wallace D. Muhammad, now known as Imam Warithudin Mohammed, brought drastic changes to the Nation. After approximately 3 years of wrestling with the changes of the teachings of the Hon. Elijah Muhammad, Min. Farrakhan after a reappraisal of the condition of Black people and the program of the Hon. Elijah Muhammad, decided to return to the teachings and the program and the proven ability to uplift and reform Blacks. This is why they hate Min. Farrakhan. They have been fighting and struggling against us from the early 40s and they thought that they had won. They thought the Nation had died and then this man stood up, backed by the Hon. Elijah Muhammad and backed by Master Fard Muhammad and brought us back to life. We need to go back and reexamine the Minister at his work. Just this morning I was reading a little book called…it's by Sis. Tynetta Muhammad, *The Comer By Night*. And she talked about Min. Farrakhan's vision in 1986 when he said, "I had a vision. I was taken up in a vision like experience to the Mother Plane and heard the voice of the Hon. Elijah Muhammad and he told me that the president, Reagan and the Joint Chiefs of Staff had come together to plan a war. And he said they would attack Colonel Muamar Kaddafi in Libya." But then he said that that war is part of a larger war which is a war against you and I. and this war will bring about Armageddon. And many thought that he'd made a mistake, because they didn't see Armageddon before their eyes. Because you see, many of you are still looking for a dragon up in the clouds. Many of you are still looking for the moon to fall and for the sun to go dark and, when you walk out of here at 11:40 for it to be like pitch-black night because you lack intellectual light. You thought that Min. Farrakhan had made a mistake. But this war continues. I read a very good book titled, "Good Muslim, Bad Muslim". This book points out how the Reagan doctrine was not one of containment but one of roll back. And he put the struggle in religion terms that he was fighting against an evil empire. So as the United States geared up to fight

147

against Russia in the Cold War, their playing ground was in the Third World. So, they supported, they formed and they financed terrorist organizations to rage acts of terror, murder and mayhem against legally constituted governments in Africa, in Angola, in Mozambique, in South Africa, in Nicaragua. So, when he saw terrorism come home on 9/11 this book says that is something that he bred himself and that the current war in Iraq, the current philosophy and program of George W. Bush is nothing but an extension of the Reaganite doctrine. And they still come together to plan a war. To plan a war overseas and to plan a war against you and me. Because foreign policy is nothing but an extension of domestic policy, so the vision is still alive. So now we should listen to the press conference of 1986 and listen to the press conference of May 3, 2004 and you'll see that the vision is still alive. The Comer By Night, are you ready for your salvation? Are you ready for your salvation? God's plan does not fail. And they plan and God plans, and God is the best of planners. They could not frustrate this plan and regardless of their intentions, their machinations of evil, our Saviour has arrived. What the Muslims Believe, point #12, "We believe that Allah God appeared in the person of Master W. Fard Muhammad, July 4, 1930. The long awaited Messiah of the Christians and the Mahdi of the Muslims. We believe further and lastly that Allah is God and besides Him there is no God and He will bring about a universal government of peace wherein we can all live in peace together." Make a decision, brothers and sisters. The Holy Qur'an says, "Then turn thy face straight to the right religion **before there come from Allah the day which cannot be averted,** On that day, they will be separated." We don't have forever! We don't know if we have tomorrow. The time is at hand.

And for those of you who are visitors and guests who may not understand enough about the religion of Islam, I want to encourage you to come anyway and join with the Nation of Islam. It takes a lot of study. It takes time to really understand these teachings, the breadth and the depth of them. And hopefully, we will continue to go deeper into the fundamental and basic teaching. Not hopefully, we will. If not on Sunday, then on Mondays or Wednesday or Fridays, in your homes, in your schools, wherever we can find you, we're going to go into these teachings so that you can understand that which has been brought to you which sets you free. But in the mean time, your Nation needs you and you need your Nation. You see, this is the flag of the Nation of Islam. This is not just a Mosque, this is an embassy. This is an embassy which is one of the headquarters of our Nation. In any Nation, you have freedom of religion. There is no compulsion in religion. The white man did not ask you if you wanted to be a citizen of his country. He passed the 13th, 14th and 15th amendments and said all persons born or naturalized in the United States are citizens. This came on the hills of 310 years of chattel slavery. And then we were proclaimed to be free. We were a people without status. But it could have gone any number of ways. The Indians have their on Nation, here on this continent of the United States. If they had given us our 40 acres and a mule, we could have found our own Nation. But they didn't ask us a damn thing, they said, "you're a citizen because you still belong to us. We removed chattel slavery, you no longer belong to an individual white man, but you belong to the government that governs the white man. You're still a slave." Come and join on to your Nation. And with that, I leave you as I came before you in the Nation's greeting words of peace,

149

As-Salaam Alaikum

WHY FOLLOW FARRAKHAN

In the Name of Allah the Beneficent, the Merciful, I bear witness that there is no God but Allah, who came in the person of Master Fard Muhammad the long-awaited Messiah of the Christians, the Mahdi of the Muslims. I further bear witness that he raised one from among us, a Georgia born Black man, the most Honorable Elijah Muhammad. He poured himself into him and made him his Messenger but more than a Messenger he has exalted him as his Christ. I further bear witness that upon his departure we were not left alone, because the Honorable Elijah Muhammad raised one and poured himself into that one, and the two of them backed this one, who is our Divine Reminder, in our midst and as he said last week, he is alive and if we are looking for a Messiah, we can call him that and that man is the Honorable Minister Louis Farrakhan and in their names I greet you in our greeting words of peace, As Salaam Alaikum

First, I want to thank Brother Eric for giving my lecture, and I leave you as I came before you. Just joking, just joking, but he pretty much did. I want to start with the call that Brother Eric made to me on Thursday, as he said, he did call me and said Brother are you ready, I want you to carry the meeting Sunday, I said what Sunday, he said this Sunday, this was like Thursday night right, and so, we hear and obey. We're always soldiers ready to be called, to be put in the game, is that right? So, I said of course Brother and then I began to think about what I would talk about. It's been quite a while since I've been here before you and I said well I'll just go back and find a lecture rework it and update and I'll be good to go, and I started going back through the lectures and nothing worked. So, I said I had been working on some themes, some things I want to write about justice and about the American justice system so I started working on a powerpoint presentation and I utterly failed. I couldn't put together anything, because it hit me that the Honorable Minister Louis Farrakhan just spoke to us last week and he is speaking to us again next week. So, I am coming in between the Minister having just spoke to us and getting ready to speak to us, what do I have to say to the people? What can I say? And I just thought about that and I realized that this is certainly not about me. There is nothing profound that I have to say. There are no pearls of wisdom that I can come up with that can outstrip what the Minister has already said and what he is going to say. I'm fairly well known for doing research, and that's my thing, I'm a lawyer, I am trained to do research. But what can I research to come in between the Minister speaking and the Minister coming up again that would be so earthshaking. I thought about it, I though what would I say to those who are here for the first time. What would I say to those who have come before but are still not sure who this man Farrakhan is? What would I say to those who have been here but sometimes, you know familiarity breeds' contempt and we get a little laxed. What is it that I would say? And what I came up with is why follow Farrakhan? So, that is the subject of my talk today, why follow Farrakhan? I think that is the number one question. That is the burning issue that we have before us today, is who to follow? Do we follow anyone, or do we follow Farrakhan, that is the most compelling question that we have to answer. It's not just who, what, when, and where but the why of it. That's the important part because if we get the why of it, then we move out with the surety. We can move out with the confidence, knowing that our decision rests on a firm basis and a firm platform. So, I don't want to lecture you today. I think there is only one man in America that is qualified to lecture us, and that is the Honorable Minister Louis Farrakhan. I want to just dialogue mentally, just share with you what Allah put on my heart to bring today. So, I don't have a PowerPoint, like I said everything I tried to do failed, even this morning I woke up and went to my office. I prepared some notes last night, typed them all out and I got ready to print it out and my laptop, my battery died. I realized I had left the battery at my office, so I got up this morning and went to my office, and I got on it and I typed it all out and got it just right and went to print it and the printer wouldn't print because the printer was out of ink. So, I said ok I will email it to myself and pull it up on my Ipad right, and when I emailed it to myself, and pulled it up on my Ipad the font had changed and I could hardly read it. I said ok, I just got to submit. It's not what Allah wants me to do so, by the grace of Allah, I just want to talk to you today, and share with you what I have on my heart and the spirit Allah had put on me when Brother Eric asked me to come before you. If I am successful in getting out of the way and allow Allah to guide this and maybe you will feel what I am feeling inside and we can make some progress.

So, why follow Farrakhan? There are political reasons. There are economical reasons. There's crime in the streets. There is police brutality and the Minister has talked to us about all of this. But there are many people vying for that space, right. You have the civil rights leaders still pushing their agendas for civil rights. You have the political self-appointed leaders who are in the season of voting and pushing the political agenda of the vote. You have the young generation coming up, you have Black Lives Matter. You have new Black Panthers and New, New Black Panthers all kinds of organizations coming up vying for the space for leadership. But I asked myself and what God put on me to talk about today is, how does God himself view the situation? And who is the leader that God has chosen and put before us and desires for us to follow. So, we don't want to look at this through the lens of economics today. We don't want to look at this through the lens of a political solution today. The Honorable Louis Farrakhan will talk to us this Sunday about the political process and what his views are regarding the vote and whole political dynamic. How does God view the situation? Does he view it at all? Does God even have a plan; is he even concerned with this? Now, there are scientist and physics scientist and theoretical scientist that study the universe, and most of them have concluded that the universe is based on what they call intelligent design. That there are laws that govern the universe. There are the physical laws; there are Newtonian laws of the physical universe, that govern the universe. We don't have to wonder will the Sun rise in the East in the morning because the universe has been set so that Earth will rotate around the Sun in such a manner that is guaranteed that tomorrow morning the Sun will in fact rise in the East, is that right? And it will, according to the laws in operation of the universe, the Sun will set again in the West. So, these are physical laws of the universe that are set by the one who is the intelligent designer of this universe. So, I pose a question to you, if this one who designed this universe with precise mathematics and science that govern it and regulate it, and makes sure the Suns don't fall from the sky and kill us all. Makes sure our planets don't deviate from their rotation and run into each other. If that one will, design the universe, according to precision and mathematical exactness, will he leave his grandest creation, man and woman, whom are called the glory of God, will he leave that to chance? So, you mean to tell me that he would design the molecular processes and chemical processes that fuel the sun that give us heat, and leave his greatest creation to wonder about without guidance. Doesn't make sense, does it? So we' would have to conclude that if this intelligent being, and the scientists, they debate with each other about the universal cosmic consciousness. Some say it's the Universal law of Karma and they have all kinds of names for it. But most agree that there is in fact a supreme being. It is this Supreme Being, that cares about our affairs. So, what kind of being would this be? Now we are taught, and there are some young people here, and young people out in the street who don't want to hear anything about religion. They don't want to hear any talk about God, and to a great extent, I agree with them, and I agree with you here to today that feel that way, because of the type of understanding we have been given about God. We've been taught that he's a spirit, a spook, that he is everywhere, and anywhere, all at the same time. But then we are also told he went forth for the salvation of his people, so if he is everywhere, why does he have to go somewhere? Doesn't make sense does it? It says that he would come from Heaven and dwell among his people. Well if he is everywhere all at the same time why does he have to come down from anywhere? Why would an immaterial spook even be concerned about the affairs of human

155

beings, who have a heartbeat, who breathe oxygen, who eat? We are told in the scripture that God has emotions, that God is a jealous God. We are told that he is an angry God at times. But on the other-hand, we are taught that we should love everyone even our enemies. So, you hear people on television when some guy walks into a church and slaughters 9 or 10 people and you hear them say, "well I forgive him", and he never even asked for forgiveness. So, if that's the kind of religion you are trying to tell me about, and many of our young people feel, that's the kind of religion you want to give me, I don't want any part of it. But that is not Muhammad's religion. We are taught that God is a man. He is a living breathing human being, but that he is the Supreme Being. But being a human being, he cares about us, his children, his family, so he intervenes in our affairs. So, having this intelligent design he would not leave us to chance. So, we are taught that there are wise men among us called scientists, and these scientists get together periodically and they study the people, the thinking, the emotions, and conditions, and with that they write up history in advance, not looking backwards but looking forward, and they compile this history and they put it in a book. In the Holy Qur'an, it says that this Qur'an is a scripture, it's a script taken from the mother book. So, there is a Master Book, a mother book, that is kept somewhere, by these scientists and through the course of human history, and based on the conditions and the needs of the people and their thinking and the reality of their conditions a part of that script is taken from the mother book and given to the people for their guidance. Because God has ordained something on himself, he says that even though he can be moved to anger, he can be so dissatisfied with the conditions and the people's response to him and to his word and to his Messengers, to the prophets, that he will utterly destroy, that people. But he said his mercy will always precede his wrath. The Holy Qur'an tells us over and over that Allah is the Beneficent the Merciful and he is the most Merciful of those who show mercy, is that right. So, before God will destroy a people he will always warn them. The Holy Qur'an says if thou had been angels, I would have sent you an angel, but since you are men, I send you a man. So, in every period when God desires to warn a people, what does he do? He goes in among that people, and raises one from among them. A man who speaks the language of that people. To give them a warning so that they don't have an excuse to say that they don't understand what he was saying, is that right. Makes sense? Ok, I am way off my topic, but like I said before, I have to go with what God has given me to say. So, we are looking at Gods plan for our salvation. How do we determine what the plan is? How do we know when we see the plan, and who the plan is coming through, so we can make the right kind of decision, because our very lives depend on it? I thank Allah for waking me this morning. I could have gone to bed last night and not seen this morning. I'm reminded of my grandmother who died, I think she was about 92; it's been some years ago, she died in her sleep. My mother told me that she she fed her and gave her, her water and put her to bed and she was in good spirit and it appeared as any other night. My mother said that somewhere during the night, she heard my grandmother says, "come by and get me", and she didn't think anything of it. She woke up the next morning to take her, her coffee and she had expired. I believe that in her sleep, I told this to my mother, I believe she saw a carriage picking up souls that had reached their rendezvous, and she said "I'm ready come by and get me." When she went to bed that night little did any of us know, we would not see her alive the next morning. So, we should all be grateful and thankful for the life God gives us every day. We should strive to make the most out of it because nothing is guaranteed. But the life that we live will be a testament to us for how we live it, long after we are gone. We can be forgotten in a moment, or our name may live on for a generation, or two, based on what we do with this life we are given. And I believe the greatest chance we have to live long is to understand God's plan, and to find that one, who he has chosen in this hour, and get with that one and be a part of that work and that mission, be a part of God's plan. Every time I get on an airplane I say "Oh Allah find some value in me, and keep this plane up, so that I can do something to aid, your will". So, I want to get a little deeper into our subject and discuss a couple of things to try to give us some perspective. I went back into my library and dug deep this time and I pulled out two books. It would behoove us to find these books, both of these are by Brother Jabril Muhammad, one is "A Special Spokesman"; the other is "Farrakhan the Traveler". So, in "A Special Spokesman", brother Jabril says, and I will read "The Honorable Elijah Muhammad teaches that there are people who have lived on several places on the Earth, whose lives and works really serves as signs of people and nations right now. A fact in their broad truth is that, to a certain extent, those people of the past, helped to shape the character, personality and therefore to a certain extent, the works of people right now. Then something of the consequences, of the actions of persons, in the past, gives some idea of what to expect in these times. History repeats itself. Many of us have heard this. Students of human nature know this and what it implies. Theologians and Historians understand and use this to help solve problems. In the course of human events, persons act from their own characteristic, from those actions flows consequences. Years later and miles from the first set of circumstances persons of similar qualities act if there are enough factors in the second set of circumstances, like the first, that will follow from the latter consequences very much like the first. So, it is said history repeats itself." So, what we see here is that Most Honorable Elijah Muhammad told us that of all of our studies, history is best suited to reward out efforts. So, we should look at history and look at circumstance and conditions of people at different periods of time, and study the actors that played on that scene, what they did, how they acted, and what were the consequences of their actions. Because, being that history is often cyclical and will repeat itself, we can identify conditions in our present time. We can identify circumstances in our present time. We can identify people, who are playing out on the stage of history in our present time that are similar to people who have played out before. Does that make sense? We can find people who have similar characteristics as to people who have impacted the course of human history before. We can find out, or we can study, the characteristics of the people, who those people came to, and what their response was, and what the resulting consequences were. So, we can study and determine the people who accepted the message. Just as well, we can study the people who rejected the message and we can identify what the consequence was of accepting the message. We can identify the consequences of rejecting the message. Does that make sense? So, we go through the Bible and we go through the Qur'an and we see stories of these ancients, and we see stories in the Holy Qur'an and it talks about the different people, the people of Salih and Thamud and we are told how Allah raised Messengers and warners and sent them to these people to address situations and the circumstances and the conditions of the people at that time. And that warner would always say "I am but a Messenger, I am a warner to you" and based on their response to the warner, based on their response, based on their response to the warning, there flowed a consequence. So, in some of these situations, we see that the people in fact, rejected the message and the consequence was destruction. And we find that when people accept the message that the consequence was that the destruction that they had earned, was delayed and they were given another chance to get it right. So, we see that the Honorable Elijah Muhammad is telling us that we have to study history, that we have to study circumstances, we have to study the people of the time, and identify the relevant characters, the relevant people who moved history forward. What were their characteristics? And we can look at our current time and we can begin to clue in to who is who, and what is what. Does that make sense? There is also something that is called types. Brother Jabril further talks about types and the signs in the types interact, plainly, they go together. I will read briefly from "Farrakhan the Traveler", and here, Brother Jabril says, "The concept embodied in the word type is essential to a good understanding of the answers to be presented in these articles. Let's work from the simple to the less simple to the more complex. It is a law, in the nature of God, which can be seen in the history of people. That whenever a people, a nation, a civilization goes so far from the divine path that destruction is their due, he always warns them. That warning comes from God through one from among them. If the people heed the teachings of the warner they are blessed. Not only is divine punishment held back but they are also guided into his ways and made successful. When people reject the divine warning, they are divinely whipped and if they persist in their evils, they are destroyed. God is consistent and just. It is only certain types of conditions that he acts which are briefly outlined above. This consistency includes the types of men he chooses to represent himself. There is also a certain sameness broadly speaking, in the characteristics of those who accept the divine message, now we are talking about the people. There is a similarity in their makeup, that more often than not, is not evident at first. The same is true of the rejecters, they are alike. It may not always seem so at first, but after a time, or when Gods judgment befalls that people, it becomes evident. The divine Messenger becomes a means, or is the chief means by which God separates the people." Let me read that again. "The divine Messenger becomes a means, or is the chief means by which God separates the people. Another way of saying this is that the people divide themselves according to the nature of their choice." So, our choice is critical today, because we are separating or dividing ourselves based on our choice, in this whole drama that is played out according to God's plan. I continue, "Now time passes, another group of people become so evil that God's nature and requirements of justice require their destruction. But his mercy takes precedence over his desire to punish. So, he selects one from among the people to warn the rest. Since he changes not, and basically evil is evil, the essential of the contents of the message to this second group of people is the same. In basic character, the man he chooses is like the rest, is like the one he mentioned, that he raised for the first group. So here we have a second situation, very much like the first in character, that is being acted up by one God who has power over the entire situation. The people who really want to improve their lives along divine lines, accept the warning. Those who don't reject him. Again, the accepters are basically alike. The rejecters are also very much alike, and they are different from and opposed to the accepters of God and his message. So, here brothers and sisters we see, there are people, circumstances and conditions that serve as a sign. A sign is not the final thing. I have a sign on the front of my office that says, Law Office of Warren Fitzgerald Muhammad. So the sign tells one, what the location is. Then it says criminal defense, personal injury, immigration, so it tells one what services are provided, but the sign doesn't provide the service. The sign only points to one who will, hopefully, Insha Allah provide the service in the right way. It points to the location where that one can be found. So, it's a sign that gives information, but it points to something else. And then there are types. And these are people who are chosen by God to function in that situation, in that condition, in that period of time, in which a warning is necessary and they demonstrate characteristics that can be identified. So, that we can look on the canvas of present time and began to identify. He has the characteristics we have seen before. She has the characteristics we have seen before, so do those who oppose them. Does that make sense? I want to discuss a number of people whose name we have heard, whom we are familiar with. I want to kind of dig down into these individuals who have played out over the course of history, and see what was it about their conditions that is similar or relevant to our condition today and what is it and what was it about those people that we may identify people who are similar to them or bear similar characteristics today. And the first man I want to deal with is Abraham. Ya'll are familiar with Abraham? Abraham is known as what, he was God's friend; he was called the Father of the Righteous. He was a black man, make no mistake about it. His people lived in the area, I think it was Ur of Chaldea and he is known as of the father of the three main branches of religion. He begat children through his wives Ishmael, Isaac and Jacob, is that right. So, over time his seeds developed into different people, but the original, Abraham, was indeed an Original Man, but he was a righteous man, he was an upright man. Upright to point that God took him into his bosom as his own friend. We are told in the Bible that Abraham sat with his friends on the plains of Mamre and God came and there was, two others with him. And he stood and told his wife to prepare them something to eat. Now this is God coming to visit his friend, and he is preparing him something to eat. That doesn't sound like a spook. Doesn't sound like a mystery, God does it? Sounds like a God who was a man, whom Abraham knew as his friend. So, we have many stories about Abraham. We have the story of, I'm going to paraphrase, I'm not a scripture quoter, but we know Abraham destroyed the idols in the Kaaba in Mecca and he went in and there were like 360 idols. There was an idol for everyday of the year. And when the leaders left the Kaaba, Abraham took a stick and smashed the idols and left one standing and when they came back they saw all the idols smashed and they wanted to punish Abraham, they wanted to kill him and they asked, who smashed the idols. He said well if he is the God, ask him. And with that he smashed idol worship, is that right. But there are two significant things that also happened to

Abraham that are relevant to our condition today and what brings us here today. One we find in the Bible, which is a dream that Abraham had. It's called a dream but I think it is more appropriate to call it a nightmare. Because the Bible says that Abraham went into darkness and a great horror. You all know what horror means. He went into a horror, a sweat in his sleep, and he saw his seed, his offspring, his prodigies down the wheel of time. And he saw that they had been taken from their own land and taken into a foreign land that was not their own. They were afflicted in that land and that they were put under hard task masters and that they would serve those task masters for 400 years. Brothers and sisters that is a long time. And these are his children. Imagine if you saw, tonight when you go to bed, you saw the demise of your child, you son, or your daughter or your nephew or your niece. You saw a horrible ending for them; imagine how that would affect you. I have grandchildren; I shudder to think if I should see their end. To being tormented, to being punished, to being lynched, to being raped, to being robbed and spoiled and this is what Abraham saw of his progeny, to the point it put him in a state of horror. But he also saw a resolution to it. God promised him that after that time, I myself will go and save that people, and I will bring them out with substance and wealth. So here God is saying that he is going to personally go and intervene in the affairs of that people of whom Abraham saw his descendants. So even though it was a nightmare he woke up with hope, is that right. Because he saw down the annuals of time that there would be these people and there would be a country that they would live in and they would be subject to this kind of treatment but there would also be salvation, that a Saviour would be sent to them. So, we also see in the Holy Qur'an, that

Abraham and Ishmael went to the Kaaba, to repair the Kaaba, which they say is the oldest place of worship on Earth. So, they didn't build the Kaaba, it was already there. But they repaired it and they said something to effect of "Oh Allah accept this from us, and accept our prayer and raise from us our offspring a nation submissive to the. I repeat, a nation submissive to the. So, they are praying for this same generation of people that Abraham, in the Bible saw, that had been enslaved and tormented, and that would ultimately get salvation. They saw this same people and prayed that Allah would raise them up as a nation, and that that nation would be submissive to Allah. That would give honor to their legacy and their history. So, we are seeing here are type, types of a person in Abraham, one who is righteous, who lives for righteousness one who stands for righteousness, one who stands to oppose the idolaters, is that right. One who breaks up polytheism and idol worship. One who has love and care and concern for his people and his children's children. So, this is giving us characteristics of one that we should look for today. One who will stand against polytheism, one who will stand against idolatry, one who will stand against the forces of evil without hesitation, without fear. Remember Abraham walked into the Kaaba by himself. With all of the priests and all of the caretakers of the 360 idols right in his midst. He walked in alone, for he knew no fear. So, these are characteristics we need to look for today. Does that make sense? So, we are going to move on to another man who came in history, and that man is Moses. So, we see Moses, another man, who knew God personally, met him face to face. God commissioned him from his face and Moses was an ordinary man. Moses didn't know the name of God, no the true God. He worshiped the

165

religion of the slave master. So here in the context of this story the people are now, slaves under a wicked task Master. The Hebrews are serving the Egyptians as the story goes and they worship the God of the Egyptians. They don't know of any other God and neither does Moses. Moses, while on a journey sees, as they say, a burning bush. He is told to take off his shoes on hallowed ground. There, God begins to dialogue with him and says, I have chosen you to go to Pharaoh and tell Pharaoh to let my people go. And Moses is looking like, Me, I can hardly talk well, not only that, I killed a man. And God says, "yes you". The Holy Qur'an says that God knows best where to place his Messengers, is that right. "You are the one that I have chosen". And I love where the Holy Qur'an says "God chose Moses, then he purified him through trial, then he gave him his mission." So, we are looking at a process, he was chosen long before he knew it. See he was born for this job. But God sent him through trials and tribulations and purified him in the furnace of fire until he got him in the right makeup. Then he called him and sent him on his way, and he told him go to Pharaoh and tell Pharaoh let my people go. Let me find in the Holy Qur'an I want to read you in Sura 7 verse 1:27 so, now Moses is now chosen for this mission. Moses does something that is very interesting, very interesting. I want to read it straight from the Qur'an, Moses said, "My Lord if you have chosen me for this mission, enlighten my mind, and make my task easy for me and remove the impediments from my tongue, so that they may understand my speech and grant me a helper from my family, Aaron, my brother. Raise my strength, through him, and associate him in my task, that we may glorify you over and over and spread your name far and wide. Surely you are indeed forever watchful over us."

The Lord said "Moses you are granted, what you have prayed for." So, here we see again a type, a type of man who is raised in a particular circumstance where his people are in a particular condition. His people are slaves to another people. His people don't know a God who has come to save them. So, he has to teach the people a new concept of God, that his name is not the name given to him by the Egyptians. He has to teach them of Jehovah, a foreign name. He has to teach them of a God who walks and talks and sees and hears, whom he met with face to face. So, what he has to teach them brothers and sisters is that is God is a man. Let me pick up the pace. And he asked God to give him a helper, in Aaron. He says that Aaron is one of eloquent speech. Are we getting some clues here? Are we starting to see how these types play out? He says that Aaron is one that the people can understand and that his voice is pleasing to them. And God says I have answered your prayers and he gave him Aaron. So, I want to move on to another man, who is again, a type. When we get to Jesus, everybody right about now, all over this country, praises Jesus, praise his Holy name, and some are jumping up and down and spinning around in circles like a spinning top and falling out on floors and I'm not trying to ridicule them, but come on, we need to study this Jesus character. So, Jesus, we know the story of Jesus, that he healed the sick and gave sight to the blind, and he fed the hungry, and he raised the dead. Now he didn't go out into the graveyard, Minister Farrakhan said you can go out into the graveyard and start preaching all you want, nobody is getting up. But the scripture he says he raised the dead and I know the story of Jesus is all too familiar to us but the point I want to get to is that, it tells us that Jesus was a sign. And we have been talking about these signs right. So, it says

Jesus was a sign. Concerning Jesus, the scripture says, "and he will appoint a Messenger to the children of Israel with a message". This is Jesus speaking and it says "I have come to you with a sign from your Lord, I have come so that I may determine for your benefit from clay a person after the manner of a bird, then I shall breathe into him a new spirit, so that he may become a flyer, a spiritual person by the authority of Allah. And I absolve the blind and the lepers and I quicken the spiritually dead, spiritually dead, by the authority of Allah and I inform you as to what you should eat, and what you should store in your houses, and behold these facts will surely serve you as a definite sign, if you are believers. I come confirming that which is before me in the name of the Torah and I declare lawful to you, some of the things that have been forbidden to you, I come to you with a sign from your Lord, so take Allah as a shield and obey me." And then another part of the Qur'an it says that Mary and her son Jesus were a sign. So again, we see that in this situation, in this circumstance, where we have one coming now to reconcile man back to God. To actually show, that man is God and God is a man, is that right. Because it was Jesus who said "what you see me do, greater things then you shall do also". He said when you see me you see the Father, which means I am in the Father and the Father is in me. So, Jesus has come to reconcile man back to God, but he too is a sign. A sign of another situation that will come down the annuals of time, of another condition of the people and of men who will be raised in that time. Ok so now we get to Muhammad, may the peace and blessings of Allah be upon him. And through Muhammad is delivered this glorious Qur'an, which came to, as a criterion, to correct the errors that had been placed in the scriptures by man's hands and to verify that which is accurate and that which is not. So, in the Qur'an it tells us that Jesus was the son of Mary and Joseph, so it dispels with this version of his immaculate birth. And it also tells us that Jesus did not die on the cross. It says no, it was made to appear that way. But surely, he did not die they killed him not, no he was raised to Allah. So, this is the defining feature of Muhammad, that he left us the book to serve as a criterion between right and wrong. And this book takes us all the way up to the present time of the hereafter. The ushering in of God's will on Earth but it does not take us all the way into the hereafter. So even Muhammad himself is a sign. He is a sign of another Muhammad. Because this Muhammad and peace and blessings of Allah be upon him, was given the book over a 23 year, period. He did not know when the next Ayat would be revealed; it would come upon him, based on time and circumstance. So, through him the book was revealed and recorded and preserved but it was not explained. See he had no one to teach him the meaning of the book. He was the one who was blessed to be the one through whom the book was revealed. But the book also talks about Muhammad being the one to warn the mother city. And being a warner to a people who had never had a warner before and that was not the Arabs. So, it's not talking about that Muhammad, it's talking about another Muhammad. We already talked about a prophet who was sent to warn the Arabs in Abraham and Ishmael when they repaired the Kaaba, is that right. Does that make sense? So, we are talking about another Muhammad, in another point in time, who will come to a people and warn that people to whom no warner had come before. That people, brothers and sisters are you and I, we are that people, that all of these signs have been pointing to, and there are people among us who are the fulfillment types of people that have been pointing to the type we should look to in this day and time. So, I want to get to my conclusion. That man that Muhammad was a sign of was and is, the most Honorable Elijah Muhammad. He's a man of the type of Abraham a man of righteousness, of fearlessness, who breaks up idolatry, who breaks up polytheism, who teaches us the one God, who stood up in America by himself and said I met with God. So, in saying that he is a type of a man as Moses. Who stands up among a people who have been in slavery and in bondage for 400 years, who fulfilled that dream that, that nightmare that Abraham had, of a people who would serve in a land not their own. So now we have a man among us a man in Elijah Muhammad, who fulfills that type as well. He's the lawgiver, he's the one who came to tell Pharaoh, let my people go, and he did lead us to the promise land. He taught us a God of a different name, one that we didn't know. He said his name was Allah and that he came in the person of Master Fard Muhammad. This was foreign to us, so he taught us a whole new understanding of the relationship between God and man, and who actually is God, and that God is a man and he cares about us. He even calls us his Uncle, is that right. Praise Allah!

So, we have this man among us who didn't speak well. We are going to wrap it up. He didn't speak well and he was a little self-conscious over the way he talked, and you all have heard the Honorable Elijah Muhammad talk. When my youngest son first heard him, he said, "Dad that's not grammatically correct", I said, "Son listen to what he is saying." Because he had a stutter and a stammering, right. But he too asked God to give me a helper. Give me one eloquent of speech.

Give me one good to look at. Give me one who is cool. Give me The Charmer, is that right. All praise to Allah! And God said I have answered your prayer. In 1955, Louis Farrakhan walked in and over time the Honorable Elijah Muhammad watched him and identified him as that one who would be his helper. So, what did the Honorable Elijah Muhammad say about Farrakhan? He said Brother Farrakhan you are worth all the wealth in the Earth. He said you are more valuable to me than 1,000 planes with a thousand head of sheep on every plane. He said you are more valuable to me than 1,000 planes, filled with gold and diamonds. Gold right now is over a $1000.00 an ounce, and you're going to fill a 747 up with gold and diamonds. He said you are more valuable to me than all of that. And he brought him out on the stage, I think it was in June of 1972, and said stand here brother, come from behind the sycamore tree. He said this is our Brother Farrakhan, where you see him, look at him. When he talks listen to him. Where he says go, go. What he says stay from, stay from. Because he is the one, when he gets you across the lake of fire, not if he gets you across the lake of fire, but when he gets you across the lake of fire, he will not say look what I have done. He will say look what Allah has done. So, who is that one we look to now? Why follow Farrakhan? Because Farrakhan is in the line of divine. And if you want to be in tune with Gods plan then you follow God's man. Now if you think yourself a God besides God then go do your thing. But if you are interested in doing what God designed for you, you will follow Gods man. I'm going to read something in closing. Ok, Brother Jabril says,

"At this point let us look at why the word "brother" rather than the word "Minister". The

171

Honorable Elijah Muhammad once said of and to Brother Farrakhan that he would rise to the pinnacle of success and honor in this worlds life. This world's life has lasted for 6,000 years and now we are at it's end. The world rejected both God and his anointed one, as we have expected. So, did our nation black people of America, this world was doomed before it was born. Not so with our nation. Nevertheless, we have rejected the opportunity of receiving an A or a B grade. However, we have a chance for a C grade through our Brother Louis Farrakhan. The C grade will save us from the D, which is the doom of this world. The authors of the signs of the Holy Qur'an 3:85 raised this question as they pondered our condition 15,000 + years ago. How shall Allah guide a people of disbelief after belief and after they had born witness that the Messenger was true? In clear, arguments had come to them. Allah guides not an unjust people only 144,000 were prophesied to escape the doom of this world by some of the wise scientists. A slim chance was outlined to save millions of our people. It's there in the scriptures; it involved the production of Brother Farrakhan by Master Fard Muhammad, the prayers of the Honorable Elijah Muhammad for the Brother, the great commission given our Brother by his teacher, before his departure in 1975. All of this and more, ultimately depended upon the exquisite execution of the divine plan given in the scripture by Master Fard Muhammad. That he brought the Honorable Elijah Muhammad into the power of bringing about. The position Brother Louis Farrakhan is growing into in this world's life reflects the position of the Honorable Elijah Muhammad in the heavens. Furthermore, it is only from the Exalted position that Brother Farrakhan can meet with and receive from the Honorable Elijah Muhammad the new teachings that will eventually bring our nation to higher grades. Finally, as you consider the Holy Qur'an 3:85 remember Allah resolved the apparent contradiction involved in the question of how shall we be guided after having rejected the Honorable Elijah Muhammad, after baring witness that he was true, in the presence of clear arguments. We have been greatly unjust to God and ourselves. However, as it is written of Allah, his strength is made perfect in weakness. From his grace, he has provided our Brother Louis Farrakhan. This act of divine grace does not come from a contradiction in his character, in the divine supreme being, no it comes from his understanding and love for us. So, let us show gratitude and help our brother our people and each other and ourselves, from unselfish interests. Let our acceptance of Brother Louis Farrakhan, be whole and not partial."

So, my dear brothers and sisters, this is why we follow Farrakhan. I Pray Allah that I have given you something of what was on my heart and on my spirit. I leave you the way I came to you in the nations words of peace.

As Salaam Alaikum.

SPECIAL THANKS

All Praise is due to Allah, who appeared in the person of Master W. Fard Muhammad. I am forever thankful and grateful for His coming and raising up His exalted Christ, The Most Honorable Elijah Muhammad, and for their finding, raising and leaving among us their reminder, The Honorable Minister Louis Farrakhan. I thank The Honorable Minister Louis Farrakhan for his standing to rebuild the work of the Most Honorable Elijah Muhammad at a time when I was lost, yet looking for Him. By making his word bond, Minister Farrakhan provided me a home where I could continue to find myself and under his guidance study these Teachings and the way of life called Islam.

Thanks to Student Regional Minister Robert Muhammad and his assistant Bro. Eric Muhammad for giving me the opportunity to occasionally speak before the people of God at Mosque 45 on the findings of my research and the messages that Allah had put on my heart. I thank the believers at Mosque 45 who demonstrated their appreciation of my efforts and encouraged me to make the contents available. I thank my sister soldier in the struggle for justice, Sister Sadiyah Karriem, for her thoughtful Foreword.

I thank my son Elijah, for being with me through my studies, questioning me, being a sounding board for my thought process and a light when I had reached periods of darkness.

I thank Sister Jeanna Hawkins for diligently transcribing and formatting the lectures.

Finally, special thanks to Sis. Stacey L. Muhammad for proofreading and editing this material.

ABOUT THE AUTHOR

Bro. Warren Fitzgerald Muhammad is a native of Acreage Homes, Texas, a black township in Harris County, which was later annexed into the City of Houston. He attended school locally in Acreage Homes and graduated from M.C. Williams Jr. Sr. High School. While in high school he was introduced to the Teachings of The Most Honorable Elijah Muhammad and began a lifelong pursuit of the course of study, of this Teaching. He is a registered member of the Nation of Islam, Mosque 45, Houston, Texas. He went on to the University of Houston, where he received his B.A. Degree in History with a concentration in Black Studies in 1976. In 1979, he became an Honored graduate of Texas Southern University's Thurgood Marshall School of Law, in Houston, Texas, and immediately went into the private practice of law. Attorney Muhammad has excelled in the practice of Entertainment Law, Criminal Defense, Personal Injury and Civil Litigation since 1979. His publications include: "This Business of Hip Hop and How to Survive", the course manual for an independently produced seminar conducted by Mr. Fitzgerald, and "The Criminal Law Survival Manual", a course manual prepared for community outreach services in Houston, Texas. In 2012, Warren Fitzgerald Jr. (Muhammad) was appointed by the Mayor as a Municipal Court Judge for the City of Houston, a position he recently resigned to focus on his law firm and private practice, and other projects under development.

Bro. Muhammad has five children with whom he maintains a close and loving relationship. He enjoys reading, writing, playing his guitar and has a movie script under development for a feature film. He is a student in the martial arts under Master William Muhammad (Soloman's Temple Martial Arts) and is a Black Belt in Taekwondo. He is a proud member of Groove Phi Groove Social Fellowship, whose mission is to "promote academic awareness and good ethical standards, to promote unity and fellowship among college men, to create intelligent and effective leadership, and to study and help alleviate the social and economic problems concerning boys and men in order to improve the stature of mankind." He has dedicated his adult life to being an advocate for the voiceless in the pursuit of freedom, justice and equality. Attorney Warren F. Muhammad can be contacted via email at wfmuhammad@mac.com.

BIBLIOGRAPHY AND SUGGESTED READINGS:

1. Holy Quran
2. Bible
3. Message To The Black Man ------ The Honorable Elijah Muhammad
4. Our Saviour Has Arrived ------- THe Honorable Elijah Muhammad
5. Fall Of America ------- The Honorable Elijah Muhammad
6. How To Eat To Live ------ The Honorable Elijah Muhammad
7. 7 Speeches ------- Minister Farrakhan
8. Torchlight For America ------- Minister Farrakhan
9. Closing The Gap ------- Minister Farrakhan
10. Self Improvement Study Guides ------- Minister Farrakhan
11. A Special Spokesman ------- Jabril Muhammad
12. Farrakhan The Traveler ------- Jabril Muhammad
13. Is It Possible The Honorable Elijah Muhammad Is Still Alive ------ Jabril Muhammad
14. The Life of Muhammad ------ Muhammad Husayn Haykal
15. Powernomics ------ Claud Anderson
16. The New Jim Crow ------- Michelle Alexander
17. The Destruction of Black Civilization ------ Chancellor Williams
18. The History of Mankind -------- Hendrik Van Loon
19. Up From Slavery ------- Booker T. Washington
20. The Book of God ------- True Islam
21. Let Us Be Muslims ------- Sayyad Maudad

22. Open Veins of Latin America ------- Eduardo Galeano
23. The Ascent of Money ------- Niall Ferguson
24. Quantum Physics and Theology ------- John Rolkin Horne
25. The Death of The Messiah ------- Raymond Brown
26. The Debt ----- Randall Robinson
27. A Brief History of Time ------- Stephen Hawking
28. A Briefer History of Time ------- Stephen Hawking
29. I Have a Dream Writings and Speeches ------- Martin Luther King
30. Islam and Revolution ------ Ayatolla Khomeni
31. The Green Book ------- Muamar Khadafi
32. Conquest By Law ------ Lindsey G. Roberson
33. The Politics of American Religious Identity ------- Kathleen Flake
34. They Came Before Columbus ------ Ivan Van Sertima
35. Black Muslims and The Law ------- Malcolm D. Crawford
36. Failed Sates ------ Noam Chomsky
37. Grand Design ------ Stephen Hawking and Leonard Milodinoa
38. The Truth of God ------ True Islam
39. The Web of Debt ----- Ellen Hodgson Brown
40. God's New Israel ----- Conrad Cherry
41. An Original Man The Life and Times of Elijah Muhammad ----- Claud Andrew Glegg III
42. Pagans in the Promised Land ---- Stephen T. Newcomb
43. Bury My Heart at Wounded Knee ----- Dee Brown
44. Mormon America ------- Ostling & Ostling

45. The Wretched of the Earth ------ Frantz Fanon
46. Native America Discovery & Conquest: Thomas Jefferson, Lewis and Clark and Manifest Destiny ------ Robert J. Miller
47. Who Is God ------ Dr. Wesley Muhammad
48. Fidel Castro: My Life ------- Fidel Castro
49. Dianetics ------- L. Ron Hubbard
50. Pedagogy of The Oppressed ------ Paulo Freire
51. The Teachings of Ptahhotep -------- Asa G. Hillard III, Larry Williams, and Nia Damali
52. The Egyptian Book of the Dead -------- E. A. Wallis Budge

INDEX

Separation, 6, 8
Sis. Tynetta Muhammad, 142
Spain, 41, 42, 43, 68
Steven Hahn, 9
Steven T. Newcomb, 74
Stokely Carmichael, 21, 137, 139
Supreme Being, 80, 149
Supreme Court, 75

T

Terra Nullius, 54, 61
Thamud, 153
The Bill of Rights, 7
The National Negro Convention, 12
Theodore Herzl, 29
Thomas Jefferson, 14, 48, 71, 72, 74, 77

Timothy Drew, 17
Traveler, 152

U

U.S. Constitution, 7
Union Army, 9
United Nations, 25, 28, 29, 56
UNITED STATES, 16
Universal Negro Improvement ndexAssociation, 17

W

White Supremacy, 38
William Wells Brown, 12
World War, 29

Made in the USA
San Bernardino, CA
25 May 2017